Hold On, Honey,
I'll Take You
to the Hospital
at Halftime

Hold On, Honey, I'll Take You to the Hospital at Halftime

Confessions of a TV Sports Junkie

Norman Chad

THE ATLANTIC MONTHLY PRESS
NEW YORK

Many of the pieces in this collection appeared originally in *The National Sports Daily* and *The Washington Post.*

Published simultaneously in Canada
Printed in the United States of America

Library of Congress Cataloging-in-Publication Data

Chad, Norman.
    Hold on, honey, I'll take you to the hospital at halftime:
confessions of a TV sports junkie / Norman Chad.
    ISBN 0-87113-557-4
    1. Television broadcasting of sports—United States.   2. Sports
spectators—United States.   3. Television viewers—United States.
I. Title.
GV742.3.C42   1994   070.4'49796'0973—dc20   93-30252

Design by Laura Hough

The Atlantic Monthly Press
841 Broadway
New York, NY 10003

First printing

To my parents,

Seymour and Perla

Contents

Introduction

It was 58 degrees outside, winds south-southwest at five to ten miles per hour, with the sun darting delightfully between partly cloudy skies. It was a mild winter's weekend of so many wonderful possibilities, from biking and hiking to walking and talking to perhaps just exploring the recesses of an ever-dulling mind.

So I watched television.

It was 68 degrees inside, a slight breeze coming out of the top of the microwave, with the living color radiating off the screen toward my pale, prone body. Clicker in hand, I went from boxing to bowling, from hockey to hoops, from recliner to refrigerator.

There was nothing to watch, there was everything to watch.

Question: Is there too much sports on television?

Answer: Let me get back to you on that one at the first TV time-out.

So there I sat, hour after hour, virtually paralyzed save for my right arm's sweeping, rhythmic motion between M&M's and mouth. *If they air it, I will watch it.* By mid-afternoon Sunday, I thought I heard the faint, familiar voice of my wife from upstairs, only to recollect that she had left several years earlier.

(Sources close to my marriage say we had a shot at making it to the five-year mark if the World League of American Football *and* ESPN baseball had not come along at the same time. "There's only so much strain you can put on the marital unit," a close, ex–family friend said. "Plus, I don't know if she ever got over that pay-per-view fight on the second night of the honeymoon." My ex-wife, living under an assumed name at an undisclosed south Florida location, declined comment.)

Sports television in the nineties is all about excess. It is about an excess of money being paid by the networks to show an excess of games. It is about an excess of replays and an excess of statistics and an excess of commercials and, always, an excess of talk. Most of all, it's about an excess of viewing on our part: It's one thing that they keep flooding us with all these games, it's another that we keep taking in the deluge until our living rooms and lives are submerged in a swamp of hopelessness.

In other words, I'm talking two TVs, two VCRs, four remotes and one ex-wife.

(Watching TV is 90 percent mental. The other 10 percent is finding the remote.)

Sports TV is all about an excess of analysts and an excess

of telestrators and an excess of graphics and an excess of sideline reporters and an excess of cameras and an excess of information and an excess of sports TV critics. I think the key word here is "excess."

Of course, where there's excess, there's ESPN.

The all-sports cable network, in fact, embodies all that is good and bad in sports TV these days. ESPN ensures, at once, that sport is taken seriously *and* that sport is taken too seriously. In smothering the sports world in hits and highlights, ESPN alternates between journalism and jingoism, between watchdog and lapdog. It raises sport to new levels while dropping civilization to new depths. One thing is for sure: ESPN should NOT be taken internally.

All roads to divorce court go through Bristol, Connecticut.

(Speaking of which, all you ever hear these days is, "There are NO good men out there." Hey, there are plenty of good men out there—they are simply IN HERE. You have to come and find us. And we're not that hard to find—we're sedentary creatures, plopped on the couch, remote in hand, future on hold. Believe me, we *are* good men, we just need somebody to get us up and out.)

You know, when we were kids, we were always told not to sit too close to the TV because it would ruin our eyes.

They were wrong.

My eyes are fine.

It ruined my mind.

Thus, I sit here these days and watch all this TV with clear vision and blurry brain waves.

(There are those who love to say, "I *never* watch television." They lie. In fact, those folks probably watch more TV than the rest of us. They're the ones who read *TV Guide,* do TV crosswords, eat TV dinners and plunk quarters into airport-terminal TVs. I watch a lot of TV, especially sports, and at least

I proudly admit it. Sure, I read, too—what do you think the commercials are for?—but when it comes down to a mid-season Pistons-Bullets NBA game or *Crime and Punishment,* I'll take Rodman over Raskolnikov every time.)

From what I can tell, there is no way around television. You could look it up—that is, if you take a moment away from taped beach volleyball to find the proper reference material, from, say, something like the *Encyclopaedia Britannica:*

> *History of the World, Part I: They invented the wheel, the printing press, the steam engine and the telegraph. They also discovered gravity, which explains why we seldom fall off the earth, and the theory of evolution, which explains a lot of other things.*
>
> *History of the World, Part II: They invented the rotary hay baler, the combine harvester and thresher, matchbook-cover advertising, single-pipe pumped-circulation heating systems and parking meters. For more recreational purposes, they also invented the nail file, the machine gun, the slide rule, the accordion, the cylinder lock, the vacuum cleaner and, of course, the zipper.*
>
> *History of the World, Part III: They invented television.*

And television's partner in cultural crime most frequently has been sports. Sports TV has come into our homes seemingly in reckless, endless fashion with slow motion and instant replay and split screens filmed by underwater cameras, hand-held cameras, wireless cameras, isolation cameras, reverse-angle cameras, minicams, MidgiCams and SkyCams. They've even attached a camera to the mask of a home-plate umpire in baseball.

Now, I'm not going to sit here and make sweeping judgments about the effect of all this televised sport on our collective psyche and spiritual development. Frankly, though, there are just a couple of ways to look at this whole existential, eudaemonistic business of who we are and why we do what we do:

(1) Life is short. Play hard.
(2) Life is short. Watch it go by.

Hey, I've made my choice.

A Revised Guide
to the History of
Sports Television

Much is made these days about the future of sports television. But one cannot truly understand the future without discovering the past, because the past often portends the present, and the present sometimes foreshadows the future, and the future, unknown as it might be, usually reflects the past. (Did I graduate from the University of Maryland with honors, or what?) So before we get along any further to where we're going, I think we have to come to grips with where we've been.

And where have we been? Through the vast wasteland* that is television in the twentieth century, that's where.

To understand where we've been, I have prepared a Revised Guide to the History of Sports Television. This guide includes significant events that predate television, events that various scholars believe had an impact on the medium. In fact, in many cases we will find that television pops up in historical periods long before many of us previously believed it existed. Incidentally, all dates in this guide have been verified by at least three independent sources, and some of the participants of these landmark events even spoke with me, although in many cases those conversations came posthumously.

So sit back and enjoy the Revised Guide to the History of Sports Television.

(Publisher's Note to the Reader: Many of the facts that follow are absolutely, positively true. Other of the facts are, well, not as true. Indeed, sometimes it is hard to distinguish fact from fiction in Mr. Chad's writing, and we actually asked him in a rather diplomatic fashion to please provide some type of guidelines for the reader to differentiate what's true and what's not—you know, maybe just an asterisk indicating those items that are real—but Mr. Chad angrily declined our suggestion. In fact, in no uncertain terms, he forbade us from making the notations ourselves, saying that we—the publisher—"better not alter one word of my stuff or I'll see you in court," a place with which the author apparently has a good deal of familiarity. In fact, it is our understanding he once sued his lawn service for cutting his grass "horizontally" rather than "vertically," and, of course, Mr. Chad's divorce-court history is a matter of very public record. Needless to say, we at Grove/Atlantic, Inc., now

---

*"Vast wasteland" is not my term. Newton Minow said it in 1962 to describe television. I'm sure he had just watched a weekend of ABC prime time.

proudly present the author's untouched, unedited, unabrogated and unauthorized Revised Guide to the History of Sports Television.)

2 MILLION B.C.: The creation of the world.

9000 B.C.: The development of agriculture begins with the growing of crops and domestication of animals in the Middle East.

4200 B.C.: People start eating dinner as a regular meal.

3600 B.C.: The wheel is invented.

3500 B.C.: The Sumerians, who live in the lower part of the Tigris-Euphrates Valley, invent the first form of writing.

1200 B.C.: Moses leads the Hebrews out of Egypt and into Palestine.

1199 B.C.: Condo prices in Palestine skyrocket with sudden overflooded real-estate market.

800 B.C.: Homer writes the *Iliad* and the *Odyssey*.

798 B.C.: Disney officials approach Homer about possible sequels to his blockbuster 800 B.C. hits.

776 B.C.: The first Olympic Games are held in Athens. No medal totals are kept, but Greek gyro carryout reports "record sales" near stadium parking lot.

612 B.C.: Babylon's most famous ruler, Nebuchadnezzar II, builds the Hanging Gardens, one of the Seven Wonders of the Ancient World. Disney officials attend opening day ceremonies to study crowd-control techniques.

586 B.C.: Nebuchadnezzar destroys Jerusalem. No film at eleven.

479 B.C.: Confucius dies. His last words: "I predict television will change the world as we know it, but pay-per-view never will realize its potential."

214 B.C.: The Great Wall of China is started. Neighboring

villages complain to local authorities about "reception problems."

202 B.C.: The Han dynasty begins its 400-year rule of China. (Now, *that's* a dynasty.)

55 B.C.: Julius Caesar leads the Roman invasion of Britain and vows "to bring English cooking into the first century."

44 B.C.: Caesar is assassinated. Brutus appears on "The Roman Empire's Most Wanted" but remains at large for two years before committing suicide near a drive-in theater.

4 B.C.: The birth of Jesus. Local media miss story, instead focusing on outbreak of gout in southwestern suburbs and upcoming croquet tournament between city councilmen and traveling midwives.

30 A.D.: Jesus is crucified. Several Good Samaritans try to save his life, but in attempting to call 911 they get busy signal for more than an hour.

395: The Roman Empire splits into the East Roman (or Byzantine) Empire and the West Roman Empire. Chariot playoffs are expanded by two teams to include "wild-card" entries from each empire.

476: Germanic chieftain Odoacer overthrows Romulus Augustulus, the last emperor of the West Roman Empire, on a late touchdown run by a reserve Heruli tribesman.

800: Charlemagne is crowned Emperor of the West; he immediately installs home entertainment center in the east wing of the castle.

1000: Leif Eriksson reaches America, but gets absolutely no media coverage.

1066: The Norman conquest of England. William the Conqueror vows "to bring English cooking into the eleventh century."

1096–99: The First Crusade is waged.

1147–49: The Second Crusade is waged.

1189–92: The Third Crusade is waged.

1202–04: The Fourth Crusade is waged.

1217–21: The Fifth Crusade is waged.

1222: America's Cup officials announce they will use The Crusades as a model for all their future competitions.

1150: The University of Paris is given its foundation charter and holds news conference to unveil plans for a 65,000-seat multipurpose stadium.

1153: The University of Paris is placed on probation for recruiting violations in its fencing program.

1271–1295: Marco Polo journeys through Asia. In an administrative foul-up, he is credited with no "frequent traveler" miles.

1337–1453: The Hundred Years' War is fought.

1492: Christopher Columbus reaches America and, ignoring the late Leif Eriksson's Sno-Kone Stand and Indian Museum plus the presence of some 3,500 Native Americans, declares himself the first man to reach the New World.

1450–1550: The Renaissance reaches its height in Italy amidst rumors of the onslaught of television.

1501: Black slavery is introduced in America. This proves to be a good deal for whites for a very long time.

1517: The Reformation begins, leading to the birth of Protestantism.

1517 (later that same year): Bingo takes hold.

1588: The Royal Navy of England defeats the Spanish Armada, establishing the British as the team to beat in Europe.

1618–48: The Thirty Years' War is fought, scaled back from the earlier Hundred Years' War to accommodate future syndication and rerun deals.

1755–63: The Seven Years' War—aimed at eighteenth-century MTV types—is fought.

1773: Angry colonists disguised as Indians board three ships and throw tea into Boston Harbor, partly to protest the British tea tax and partly to protest bad British cooking. The colonists are helped by some questionable calls from Boston officials.

1789: The French Revolution, brought upon largely by feudal oppression and poor cable service, begins.

1791: The Bill of Rights is added onto the U.S. Constitution. Congressional leaders consider an amendment guaranteeing Americans the right to watch all sports on free TV, but the legislation dies as Thomas Jefferson implores, "No one has television. What the hell are we talking about?"

1803: The United States purchases Louisiana from France for $15 million and a truffle to be named later.

1812: The War of 1812 is fought. Originally it had been scheduled to be the War of 1811, but production and cost overruns delayed the start for one year.

1815: Napoleon Bonaparte is defeated in the Battle of Waterloo, ending his attempt to rule Europe and establish a twenty-four-hour all-monarchy news channel.

1823: The Monroe Doctrine is enunciated, stating that the American continents are no longer open for colonization by European powers and that the 8:00 to 11:00 P.M. period nightly would be set aside for "prime time" entertainment for all American settlers.

1849: The California gold rush begins.

1849 (later that same year): Two game shows, "Strike It Rich" and "You Don't Say," debut in southern California.

1854: The Kansas-Nebraska Act is passed, repealing the antislavery clause of the Missouri Compromise, creating the Kansas and Nebraska territories and establishing a home-and-home football series between the two rival states-to-be.

1861–65: The Civil War is fought, effectively ending black slavery. Whites adjust accordingly, turning to other arenas—particularly boxing, college basketball and chauffeuring—in order to continue exploiting black labor.

1869: The Suez Canal is opened. Local officials promise it will be wired for cable "by the end of the century."

1895: Guglielmo Marconi invents radio telegraphy. (Years later, after hearing "The Howard Stern Show," he issues a public apology.)

1898: The United States takes control of Guam, Puerto Rico and the Philippines following the Spanish-American War, creating several new Nielsen cities.

1918: Howard Cohen, later known as Howard Cosell, is born, marking the unofficial start of the sports television era.

1927: Charles Lindbergh makes the first nonstop solo flight across the Atlantic. The in-flight movie: Buster Keaton's *The Navigator.*

1929: The U.S. stock market crashes, bringing on the first Great Depression.

1939: The first major league baseball game (Reds vs. Dodgers) is televised on station W2XBS in New York City.

1939: The first pro football game (Eagles vs. Dodgers) is televised on station W2XBS in New York City.

1940: The first hockey game (Canadiens vs. Rangers) is televised on station W2XBS in New York City.

1940: The first college basketball game (Pittsburgh vs. Fordham) is televised on station W2XBS in New York City.

1940: A coalition of New York City housewives petitions Federal Communications Commission to revoke station W2XBS's license.

1940: The Battle of Britain is fought during World War II. Germany unsuccessfully attempts to bomb Britain into submission as Adolf Hitler vows "to bring English cooking into the twentieth century."

1953: Color telecasts begin, leading to the advent of color analysts.

1955: Chris Berman is born, bringing on the second Great Depression.

1959: Fidel Castro wins control of Cuba on promises of "a new social order" and "unscrambled signals" of American TV police dramas.

1961: "Wide World of Sports" debuts on ABC as just a summer replacement series, but it turns out Jim McKay can't get a Saturday off for the next thirty years.

1963: During the Army-Navy football game, CBS uses "instant replay" during a live telecast for the first time. Bob Trumpy calls Tim McCarver and tells him, "There are jobs for us in TV when our playing days are over."

1969: American TV viewers apparently watch the first man land on the moon. In a little-known pact between NASA and Ralph Edwards, though, the moon sequence actually is filmed entirely at Universal Studios in Universal City, California.

1970: "Monday Night Football" debuts on ABC, without Frank Gifford.

1971: Frank Gifford joins "Monday Night Football," and it turns out sensible viewers can't have peace of mind on Monday nights for the next thirty years.

1979: ESPN goes on the air, the seventh sign of the apocalypse.

1980–89: There is an explosion of sports television in America, not unlike the violent 1883 volcanic eruption of Krakatoa in western Indonesia that darkened skies over vast areas, scattered debris as far as Madagascar, swept over coastal areas with vicious force and engulfed entire civilizations.

1990–current: Remember, it is always darkest before the dawn.

Frankly—and This Is Just My Opinion— You Shouldn't Watch Sports on TV

I turned on "Love Connection" the other day. It's not all that good, but I watch, see which dates don't work out and then call the appropriate women to catch them on the rebound.

This is my life. This is all of our lives. We are The Children of Television, and when your parents are a bunch of cathode-ray tubes with a history of electromagnetic radiation problems, your outlook on the world is going to be a bit blurry.

But today, I want to reach out to someone other than Chuck Woolery for help. I want to share my pain of watching so much television. I want to plead for a new day, one in which entire lives don't revolve around a 19-inch mechanical companion. I want us all to see the light on the dangers of sitting lamely at home, watching our lives pass us by one game at a time.

Most of all, I just want my shrink to cut his three-week vacation short and see me immediately.

I became a sports television critic in 1985. These are the changes that the eight-year stint have wrought:

	1985	1993
Age	26	unsure
Height	5-foot-9	5-foot-8½
Weight	163	282
Eyes	Blue	Red-rimmed
Hair	Brown	Pulled out
Marital status	Married	Divorced
Will to Live	Strong	Flagging

These are the days and nights of my life:

I was watching ESPN at 4:00 A.M., seduced into a hypnotic state of inertia. My body demanded sleep, but my mind refused to act. I sat there, deadened. I sat there, staring at indoor soccer. I sat there, not even knowing I was sitting there. I heard nothing, I saw nothing, I felt nothing. I simply watched. My eyelids wouldn't close. This was a cable lobotomy, a clean and painless cut. I had yielded control of my life. I came, I saw, I surrendered.

Like a good flophouse, sports cable is a twenty-four-hour-a-day operation, full of cheap and empty pleasures. Sports television, I have found, cures restlessness, loneliness and consciousness, all from the convenience of your living room. It creates a psychic undertow of sorts; you're not quite aware that you're drifting into a mental mausoleum.

Thanks to sports television, I have the attention span of a mosquito. From the days in which I once read long novels, I now get fidgety halfway through the back of a cereal box. It's not just me; it's everyone. We talk less, we read less, we think less, we live less. When you combine the cable boom with the VCR craze, you get a republic that considers *TV Guide* serious reading. From the Fuji Blimp, you might see 100 million homes filled with 250 million people in front of 300 million TV sets. One nation, under God, indivisible, with Lite beer and just programming for all.

TV is our so-called window on the world, but in actuality, we've drawn the shades and locked ourselves into terminal darkness.

For a generation of sports fans, life is a wireless remote. Exercise? My idea of a training regimen these days is to watch "30-Minute Workout" in fast-forward—while lying down.

Because of sports television, I lost perspective on my family life and subsequently—rightfully so—lost my family. Here, for instance, is a sample conversation between my then-wife and myself on a Sunday afternoon in November 1986.

"Hey, Norman, can you come into the kitchen for a moment?"

"Yeah, I'll be there in a minute."

(Five minutes go by.)

"Honey, it's an emergency. I need to see you."

"The Steelers are driving, for crying out loud. Give me a minute."

"Well, I badly cut open my hand here shucking these clams. I can't get the bleeding to stop. I'm feeling awful faint, Norman."

"OK, listen. It's third-and-six. Uh, how bad is it?"

"It's pretty bad."

"OK, then, we're coming up on the two-minute warning.

Throw the damn ball out of bounds!! Uh, I'll call the hospital then, and I'll take you over at halftime."

"I think we might want to go now."

"Just hold your hand under cold water and lean up against the counter. If they don't make this fourth down, we'll go then."

(The Steelers made the fourth down, and I took my wife to the emergency room at the half, where she received seventeen stitches in her right hand. The waiting room, unfortunately, had a different game on. The aforementioned conversation, incidentally, was introduced as key evidence at a pretrial hearing, known better as *Chad* v. *Chad*, which determined that the two of us would no longer be, well, together. And, sure, I know the book cover shows my wife to be pregnant when this incident occurred, but that never happened. My publisher insisted we exaggerate a bit on the cover because he thought a cut hand wasn't dramatic enough to sell a lot of books. Besides, the possibility of any pregnancy during my marriage was greatly reduced by one of my wife's long-standing policies, which can be summed up in five words: "Stay away from me, Norman.")

So now I come to you today both to share my misery and to finally do my duty.

I am here to help save the republic. I am here to tell you, as a professional sports television critic and fellow American: Don't watch sports TV. Don't ever watch it again.

Step 1: Toss the remote out.

Step 2: Toss the TV out.

Step 3: Scan the wedding and engagement announcements in your local paper; maybe you can persuade somebody's fiancée to change her mind.

By the way, "Divorce Court" is on USA cable nightly.

Could You
Please Be Quiet?
I'm Trying to Watch
the Game.

Imagine the following:

You're watching the final scene of *La Bohème* on PBS. The consumptive Mimi, with lover Rodolpho and other friends by her side, tries to warm her cold little hands. As she coughs incessantly and breathes a final breath of life, PBS opera analyst John Simon offers, "Mimi is dying of consumption. AND RODOLPHO DOESN'T EVEN NOTICE!! Oh, wait, now he sees, now he notices. And now—take a look at this—somebody is talking with Rodolpho . . . yes, yes, somebody is telling him to have courage at this tender moment. Let's listen in."

Or . . .

You're watching the climactic stages of *Dirty Harry* on ABC. Detective Harry Callahan is in pursuit of the sniper who calls himself Scorpio. Scorpio has terrorized San Francisco for weeks, leaving a trail of death behind him, and as Callahan and his .44 Magnum finally close in on the criminal, ABC film commentator Robert Blake breaks in, "Hey, I've been in this situation a dozen times, lemme tell ya. I don't think Harry's gonna bring him in, I think he shoots him without question. He's gotta! Violence begets violence, baby. I mean, when we did 'Baretta,' you wanna avoid the shootout if you can, but this guy's been such a pain in the caboose to Harry, I think Harry just blows him away. Bang, bang—just like that."

If this were the way it was, a lot of wonderful theater and film productions would be diminished as we watched them. Well, unfortunately, that's the way it is when sporting events are televised, so a lot of wonderful games are diminished as we watch them.

Yes, the No. 1 problem for viewers of sports television remains a simple one: The announcers won't shut up.

They repeatedly tell us what just happened or what's about to happen, and in either case, we usually can see what's happening for ourselves.

This, however, is a problem that cannot be stopped as easily as it can be spotted. After all, put a nut in front of a squirrel and he eats it; put a prescription in front of a druggist and he fills it; put a microphone in front of a broadcaster and he speaks into it.

But the time has come for broadcasters to adjust to a more sophisticated viewing audience and to an ever-advancing technology. Consider that improvements in sports television over the past generation—better camera angles, slow motion, attractive graphics, up-to-the-minute statistics and superb audio—have made our living rooms the best seat in the stadium. And yet sportscasters continue to talk over the action and over the scene.

In many cases, for all the announcers' talk-is-cheap chatter, nobody cares to listen. TV sports viewers can be divided into two general categories: detached, rational people who are watching a game without a particularly strong rooting interest, and highly partisan fans who favor one team or the other. When a game reaches its pinnacle, the detached viewers want to soak in the atmosphere—the players' reactions, the coaches' maneuverings, the fans' mania—and don't want an announcer shouting at them. Meanwhile, the partisan rooters react to a game's biggest moments by yelling at their family and friends, and thus hardly ever hear the announcers' ramblings.

Both play-by-play broadcasters and jock analysts are guilty of too much talk. Many lead announcers insist on giving a radio play-by-play on TV games. When we see a ball hit to left field, they tell us it's hit to left field. When a graphic is put up reflecting a tailback's total yardage, they repeat the figure for us. When the scoreboard clock is shown, they tell us how much time is remaining. We continually are told what we already know.

Meanwhile, analysts often are victimized by overproduction. Many producers relish showing too many replays of meaningless action or endless angles of the same play, which in turn encourages the analyst to analyze and overanalyze. If ex-playwrights aren't compelled to sit around and explain Willy Loman to us in the midst of *Death of a Salesman,* then why must ex-coaches exclaim endlessly about full-court presses on ESPN's Big Monday? Are zone defenses really more complex than the human condition?

Adding to the problem is ABC's Monday night mentality of overcrowding the booth. In simple math, 1 + 1 + 1 = 3. But in broadcast math, 1 + 1 + 1 = too many. With so much competition for airtime, there's seldom dead air. Almost every broadcast these days uses a disguised three-man booth with "sideline reporters," who are as often intrusive as informative.

It's become trendy in recent years for announcers to go silent at game's end, to let us soak in the sights and sounds for a few moments. This sensible approach should prevail prior to the final gun as well. Like a gripping drama unfolding on stage, a tense, taut game becomes all the more compelling when a broadcast lets it develop without diversion. Still, in most cases, just when we think the picture says it all, we find out the announcer has a little something to add.

One solution, of course, is for viewers to turn the volume off. It might give a new twist to an age-old riddle—if an announcer does play-by-play and nobody's listening, does he make a sound?

"It's Alivvve!! Gimmmmee the Rockkkk!!!"

Along the streets of America often comes this screeching, blaring sound, a harsh, horrific honking that shatters the senses. An automobile horn is stuck, you assume. Then again, it just might be Dick Vitale.

His is a high-pitched, piercing voice with no sense of dimension, an endless, eerie seasonal shrill that celebrates hype and hysteria. Vitale is an attack analyst, not so much discussing college basketball for ESPN and ABC as demolishing it. Trying to listen to a Vitale telecast is like trying to catch a speeding bullet with your teeth—the risks far outweigh the rewards.

I am a founding member of the burgeoning grass-roots video advocacy group If Dick Vitale Ever Enters My Living

Room via ESPN Again I Will Not Watch College Basketball on TV for the Rest of My Natural Life, popularly known by the acronym IDVEEMLRVESPNAIWNWCBOTVFTROMNL or, more simply, NOMOREVITALE.

We're tired of helplessly sitting down in front of the TV set for a game and getting run over by halftime. Our motto is: Friends Don't Let Friends View Vitale.

Since 1979 on ESPN (and since 1986 on ABC), Vitale has shouted and screamed and shucked and screeched and squealed and squalled. It's a one-note act, and it's played over and over. When Vitale does his shtick in the studio, it's relatively fun and harmless, if a bit tiresome. But during game telecasts, Vitale's hype is hazardous; he doesn't complement a game, he competes against it.

The effect on the viewer is disorienting. It's like trying to relax out on your back porch and listen to Mozart's Piano Concerto in B Flat while someone next door is mowing the lawn. Vitale's voice could peel the skin off a potato, and when he's on one of his shrill rolls, he only brakes for small animals and commercials.

Vitalespeak, which combines elements of several dead languages, is virtually impossible to understand. He is the human Rorschach test. Worse yet, Vitale seems to be spawning a generation of imitators, most notably Bill Raftery, who has gone from being a mediocre basketball analyst to a maddening one. (Not only do I think Raftery talks in his sleep, I believe he actually dreams in color commentary.)

But, hey—let's let Vitale shriek for himself. Let's roll the tape on Vitale during several telecasts. Here, then, the unexpurgated Dick Vitale:

- "He [Northwestern's Rex Walter] sat on the pine last year. This year, he's leading the Big Ten in scoring. He's going to have to stroke the 'J' . . . I don't know about you, *I'm pumped up*. I love when the little guy, David and Goliath. Everybody here's excited. *The zoo crew!!* Everybody can't wait. Are you excited? *Let's play ball, baby!!*"[1]

• After little-used substitute David Bartelstein comes in for Syracuse: "Hey, David! C'monnn, D.B. *Look at my little guy!!! Look at D.B. C'monnn, baby!!! Look at D.B.* A little shake 'n' bake. *C'monnn. I want to see him score!!!*"[2]

• After a dunk by Syracuse's Derrick Coleman against Villanova: "Ohhhhhhhh, but they don't have Derrick Coleman [at Villanova]. But they don't have *The Monnnnnnssster Massssher!* And they love him! They say, 'Please stay here for another year, Derrick, please stay here for another year.' [Replay starts.] There's the pass and [David] Johnson. *Take a look, baby!!! Binnnnnggggo!!* And Billy [Owens] says, 'I love you, Derrick.' That was in-your-face, get-out-of-my-way, *I'm-taking-this-baby-home!!!*"

• After Syracuse's Stephen Thompson scores at the first-half buzzer: "Ohhhhhhhh!!! They score. Count it! Count it! Stevie Thompson with the great legs, the jumpin' jack. Smile, [Jim] Boeheim. C'mon and smile, Proffffessssssor!!!"

• As Syracuse routs Villanova: "C'mon, Jimmy, c'mon, Jimmy, get Sherman [Douglas] out of the game. You don't want to chance an injury. Get him sitting next to ya!! [Interrupts partner Tim Brando.] C'mon, Jimmmmy, c'mon, Jimmmmmmy, look down the bench, let those kids that

---

[1]Vitale generally gets excited on air before every game, regardless of the matchup.
[2]Vitale often takes over play-by-play chores. In this sequence, he is describing Bartelstein dribbling the ball.

practice all the time get some P.T. *C'monnn, James Boe-hhhheimmm!!!"*[3]

- "Uh-oh, there's the steal. Billy Aussstinnn was Mr. Basket-ball in Indiana. . . . Get a T.O., Bill Foster. *Get a T.O.!!! And he gets the T.O. He gets the T.O. down nine, Timmmmmmy Beeeeee!!!!"*[4]

- Midway through a West Virginia–Kentucky game: "Won-der if John Saunders can shoot the three? I bet he'd get nothing but air ball. I don't think he can shoot the three! *I don't think he can even get near the rim!* . . . I know Chris Berman can't shoot the three. Berman's a definite post man. He's a member of my all-wide body team, *Misssstter Chris Beeeeeee!!!"*

- After ESPN shows a student holding up a Vitale-for-Presi-dent sign: *"Watccch out, George Busssshhh. . .* They were great to me today at the book signing we had down on the campus. The place was jammmmmmed. I had loads of fun. *Currrry Kirkpatrick would've been on cloud ninnnne to be there!!!* I couldn't sign all the books for all the kids. I didn't have enough time and enough books, basically. No, we had the books. I didn't have the time."[5]

- "Is he a big-time player? Hey, America, get used to it—Steve Smith is a big-time player. Montgomery scores the deuce, but the finnnalizzzer, the guy who made it hap-

---

[3]Vitale often shouts directly to coaches and players, forgoing the tradition of many of his broadcast and print colleagues, who prefer to wait until after the game to talk with the participants.
[4]One team is apparently rallying here, and Vitale is informing his play-by-play partner, Tim Brando, of the development.
[5]Vitale is the author of a book, mostly in English, entitled *Vitale.*

pen—Steve Smith of Michigan State. . . . Look at Smith right now. Here he comes—a little shake 'n' bake. He says, 'I'm going to make like the Magic Man. I'm going to look one way. *Hey, Magic, did you throw a pass like that?* He says, 'Hey, Greg Kelso, sitting up there doing the game on radio: Did Magic throw it to you like that, baaaabbbbby??!!' " [6]

- After Illinois beats the Iowa press and scores on a fast break: *"That's what I mean about finnnalizzzin', baby!!!"* [7]

- After Iowa scores several straight points against Illinois: *"Time-out! Get a time-out, Loooou Hennson!! Get a T.O., baby!! Get a T.O., LOOOU. YOU BETTER GET A TIME-OUT!!"* [8]

- As camera shows Illinois coach Lou Henson: "He's got his LooooouDooo in place today!! He was teasing me about my DickieDoooo. . . . [Iowa coach] Tom Davis's first six games in the Big Ten were on the road. He was like Marco Polo, playing all those road games. [9]

- "Look at Lou Henson, he can't belieeeeve it. Watch out, his LooouDoooo is going to fall out. C'monnnn, Lou, don't get so excited!! *Don't get so frustrated, Loooou! Watch the*

---

[6] Apparently, Steve Smith is playing well. Then again, the arena could be under a Russian nuclear attack at the moment.

[7] Among the innumerable linguistic Vitalisms is his insistence that players do not "score" at the end of fast breaks; rather, they "finalize" (from the Latin *finalitas*—to bring to completion an act of scoring).

[8] Vitale's favorite form of direct, on-court communication is to instruct coaches to take a time-out. They often do, which then allows the viewer the relative serenity of a sixty-second commercial break.

[9] A rare reference to the noted Venetian traveler (1254–1324) in eastern Asia, who, despite his extensive journeys, never saw a Division I college basketball game.

Loooudoooo, it's moving!! C'MONNNNNN, LOOOU, CALM DOWN!!'"[10]

- Illinois' Ken Battle dunks: "Ohhhhhhhh, uhhh-ohhhhhhhh!!! *Flight Nummmmber Thirty-three!! The Flying Illllinnni!! Kennnny Battle!!* Hey, I think we're right now over at the Rucker League in New York City. *Run, baby, run!!!* But you know, the fans love this style of play. They really love the athliti—athleticism—is that the word?"

- As Iowa and Illinois players scramble for a loose ball: "Hey, Hayden Fry—look at [Iowa football coach] Hayden Fry on the sideline. He wants to sign these guys. *It's recruiting time!!* Fry says, 'Let me get some of these athhhh-e-letes.' Tom Davis says, 'You caaaannnn't havvve them, Hayden. . . . You know, Hayden Fry started—you want a little story?"[11]

Now, I could go on and on detailing Vitalespeak's ills—his shrill sounds, for instance, are often confused with the mating call of the Tasmanian wombat—but I thought it might be nice, for a change of pace, to sort of celebrate the master shillman's style. That's right—let's suspend reality for a moment (as if we don't when we're listening to him normally) and consider Vitale had he been around to expatiate on other earthly pursuits. And so, without further pause, here is Dick Vitale as witness to Great Moments in History:

---

[10]This apparently is the classic case of the pot calling the kettle black.
[11]Ohhhhhhhhhh, no.

Moses Delivers the Ten Commandments

"Here he comes, he is mul-TI-dimensional. What can you say, Keith—he's a diplomat, a military chief, a lawmaker, a politico, a judge, a religious and spiritual leader, a PTPer on God's team. What a club the G Man has put together—they're number one in AP, UPI, CNN, nobody beats this team, home or on the road. Take that, Duke Blue Devils! And what a point man Moses can be—great, great peripheral vision.

"Let me tell you quickly: He was born during a bad time, his mother hid the baby in a basket off the bank of the Nile River—one of the best rivers in the Middle East—the Pharoah's daughter finds Moses and raises him! Just a great, great recruiting story! And then, of course, the whole parting-of-the-Red-Sea thing—unbelieeeeevable!

"And now, he's descending Mount Sinai with those stone tablets. He's got to square his body or he's gonna drop 'em! Ohhhhh, he does drop them! He turns over the Ten Commandments! Uh-ohhhhh—I can see number seven there on the ground, 'Thou shalt not commit adultery.' The rules committee will have to take a good look at that one . . ."

Columbus Discovers America

"What a great seeeeeaman, what a great explorer. He's provin' the world ain't flat, baby. They call him Cristóbal Colón in Spain, but he's just C.C. here. He made just one mistake—he underestimated the width of the Atlantic. Bad scouting, baby.

"But what a great, great hire for King Ferdinand and

Queen Isabella. And what a great deal The Admiral got—three ships at royal expense, a share of the trade, noble rank, governorship of any land he might discover. EAT YOUR HEART OUT, VASCO DA GAMA!!!

"He's got te-NA-city. Aw, Keith, the toughest wind in navigating to defend is the back wind. *What a job The Admirrrral has done!* He had a little dissension on board, a few guys on the pine unhappy with being below deck, looking for some A.T.—air time—but C.C.'s got the good compasses, the smooth seas, the steady hand on board.

"Uh-ohhhhhhhhhh! He's struck land! *Aw, look at the Indians chanting, 'Rock Chalk, Jay Hawk!!!'* But Christoppppher Colummmmmmbus is the man of the hour. Mark it on your calendarrrr—it's Colummmmmmbus Day! The Columbus crazies love it! He's the VICEROY OF THE INDIES! Colonize, baby, colonize!"

Custer's Last Stand

"You've got to like the chances of The Boy General, one of my Diaper Dandies, George Armmmmmstrrrong Custer. I talked to The General yesterday, and he figures these Sioux and Cheyenne could be pushovers. We're talkin' Blowout City!

"The General's gonna attack immediately! But who are these Indians? There must be two thousand of them. *Here comes the pressure!* Aw, it's physical out there! No! C'mon, don't call that! *What a bad call!* I thought he beat him to the spot, but they're saying Sitting Bull got there first. This is unbelieeeevable!!!! They're beating up The General! CUSTER'S GOT NO LUSTER!!! Poor spacing, Keith, poor, poor spacing. The cavalry is retreeeeating!!! Time-out! GET A T.O., GENERAL GEORGE,

GET A T.O., BABEEEEEEEEE!!!!! Where's the ground support? Crazy Horse has given the Indians some quality minutes. GET A T.O.!!

"Down goes The General! Down goes The General! Little Bighorn is rockin'! These Indians are gonna get out of here with a W! It's rock 'n' roll time at Bighorn!!! IT'S OVER, BABY!"

The First Man on the Moon

"And they land that—whatcha call it, Keith—a lunar module? The Apollo Nummmmber Eleven loooooonar module. And now let's see if Neil Armstrong has that quick first step for a man . . . HE'S ON THE MOON! One small step for man, one giant leap for the Big Ten! Is he Mr. Clutch? IS HE MR. CLUTCH? He says, 'It's my time, it's showtime!' You've gotta know they're proud in Wa-pa-ko-ne-ta, O-HIII-o. Purdue grad. Navy pilot. Flew combat missions in Korea.

"It's a tremendous environment out there. There's the good look. He's putting on a show, Keith. He's a skywalker, he plays above the stars! That's awesome, baby, with a CAPITAL A!

"He's got the rock! *He knows what to do with the rock!* BRING IT ON HOME, NEIL, BABY! GET THE ROCK TO EDDIE ALDRIN! GET IT TO EDDIE! C'MON, NEIL!!!"

I Once Had
a Remote and a Wife.
I Still Have
a Remote.

Yeah, I was married once for a little while. (As they say in baseball, I was up for "a cup of coffee" in the big leagues of matrimony. Actually, as I recall it, I had asked my wife one day to make me a cup of coffee and she told me to make it myself and I reminded her of our proper spousal roles and she told me I was living in a social time warp and I made a few ill-advised comments regarding her family and the next thing you know, we're in District of Columbia Superior Court determining that we'd prefer *not* to wait till death do us part.)

So now I'm divorced. (Actually, I prefer to think of myself as "between marriages.") And the most frequent question I'm asked is: "What went wrong?"

Well, we once went to a marriage counselor to find out what was going wrong, and she promptly told us: "Couples having marital difficulties usually are having problems in one of three areas—money, sex or communications."

We stared back at her blankly.

"So which is it?" the counselor asked.

"The biggest problem," my wife and I responded in unison, "is the remote."

I want to make myself perfectly clear on this issue because, frankly, I believe I always have been on the forefront of feminism in this country and I've loudly supported equal rights and I've been as enlightened and progressive on women's issues as any football-loving, natural-selection male survivor can be. But when it comes down to the matter of women and TV, I simply must take what will be viewed by many as a retrogressive, reactionary stand.

Seventy-odd years ago, we gave them The Vote.

Now, they want The Remote.

To which I say: Hell No, We Won't Let Go.

Once the marriage counselor realized we were serious about our clicker conflict, she let us vent our frustrations. We spent our entire first hour—well, actually, fifty minutes, that is, because when you "pay by the hour" in the psychiatric community, you get only fifty minutes on the clock, a curious therapeutic policy that deserves further inspection by various consumer-rights groups, if you ask me—complaining about each other's remote habits.

I can highlight the hour—excuse me, again, I mean the fifty minutes—by relaying to you the following statements made by my ex-wife and myself:

Her: "He gets the thing in his hand and he goes from game to game, from game show to game show, from sitcom to drama, from MTV to TNT, all around the entire dial in sixty seconds or less. He doesn't watch anything longer than a moment or two. We always see one three-point basket or one line of dialogue or one stanza of a song. I've never seen a contestant give the right question on 'Jeopardy'; all we see is the category flash up. I've never even seen who hosts 'Jeopardy,' and we watch parts of it every single day. He's got the attention span of a moth. Actually, come to think of it, his skin color is very mothlike lately."

Me: "The goddamn broad will watch an entire thirty-minute infomercial for The Atomizer without switching the channel even once."

It was safe to say that, on this one issue alone, we had what is politely called "irreconcilable differences."

Obviously, the bottom line was: We both wanted the clicker, and neither one of us could stand the other to have it.

Game. Set. Marriage.

(At this point—for the sake of fairness—I'd like to introduce facts from a recent university study that suggest a root cause of marital discord other than The Remote. Of course, I firmly believe The Remote caused my marriage to tumble, but according to University of Denver psychologist Howard Markman, baseball could've played a pivotal role. Markman, director of the school's Center for Marital and Family Studies, published a report that concluded that "going to a baseball game could save your marriage." According to Markman's study, cities with major league teams have a divorce rate 23 percent lower than cities without teams. Now, even though I don't trust any university study of any kind—plus we're talking about a psychologist here, who undoubtedly believes that fifty minutes equal one hour—let's assume for a moment that Markman's findings are legitimate. Well, I can't tell you how sad and disheartening it is to find out this scientific conclusion a scant three years after my own divorce became final. Because, indeed, my ex-wife and I were married in Washington, D.C., we lived in Washington, D.C., and we were divorced in Washington, D.C.—and, as we all know, Washington, D.C., tragically has been without a major league baseball team since the Senators were unceremoniously yanked out of town in 1971. If I had simply been aware of this relationship between baseball attendance and marital success at the time of my wedding, we would've moved to Baltimore in a New York minute. I WANT TO KNOW WHO I CAN SUE, and you damn well better believe I hope the legal action includes those short-timing shrinks everywhere they may be.)

Anyway, recently I began seeing someone seriously for the first time since my divorce, and we were getting along swimmingly. So we're sitting in my apartment one night watching "Northern Exposure"—it was our second date, so I thought it okay to make it a TV evening—and everything's going fine.

Until the commercial.

She got up to pour herself a cup of coffee—which, I might add, I made—and by the time she got back, I had switched to the Oklahoma-Oklahoma State basketball game on ESPN.

"What happened to the show?" she asked, somewhat irritably.

"I just wanted to check out the score on this one game," I responded, somewhat amicably.

"Oh, no," she said. "You're not going to watch this crap."

"But it's Big Monday!" I exclaimed.

She took the clicker out of my hand—I mean, she grabbed that baby—and switched back to CBS. When "Northern Exposure" ended, she got her coat and told me she was walking out forever.

I pleaded with her to stay, at least through "SportsCenter." But she simply thanked me for the coffee and left. Alas, I still had the clicker.

On "Monday Night Football," Three's a Crowd

"Are you ready for some footbaaahhhlllll?"
—Hank Williams, Jr.

In a word, no.

There's a problem with ABC's "Monday Night Football."

To put it in strictly physiological terms, it pertains to, and is concerned with, and is measured by an inundation or deluge of the sensorium, otherwise known in academic and medical circles as "sensory overload."

To put it in strictly English terms, the damn announcers won't shut up.

This is a shame, because there is much that is good about ABC's "Monday Night Football," not the least being that in the increasingly overcrowded sports-TV marketplace, it remains the one week-to-week show that even jaded fans can look forward to with anticipation and excitement.

And the whole "Monday Night Football" production has many outstanding aspects, including: The games look visually sensational; director Craig Janoff and producer Ken Wolfe are solid in their use of the dozen or so cameras; director of information Steve Hirdt provides incomparable statistical graphics; play-by-play broadcaster Al Michaels is forever refined.

However . . .

(At this point, we're going to have to ask all ABC Sports employees and their families to please leave the room, partly because of the blunt, explicit nature of what follows and partly because it's easier to talk about you behind your backs.)

OK, then, who's the corporate clown that gave the go-ahead to this whole Hank Williams, Jr., thing?

The insufferable "All My Rowdy Friends" theme and its musical cousins set a bawdy, boorish tone to the evening. It's loud and it's ugly. Sure, for all I know Hank Williams, Jr., may have played at Keith Jackson's wedding reception, but that doesn't qualify him for national overexposure. ABC would be better off with Roseanne Arnold doing something *a cappella.*

But Williams's in-your-face, party-till-it's-over, strut-your-stuff style is a minor nuisance compared to the broadcast's three-in-the-booth bombardment. The song, after all, lasts only forty-five seconds; the game's with us for three hours.

In the mid-1980s, ABC approached disaster in the booth. Bottom was reached in 1985, as misplay-by-misplay broadcaster Frank Gifford was joined by two horrendous jock analysts, O. J. Simpson and Joe Namath. So in 1986, new ABC Sports president Dennis Swanson brought in Michaels as the lead announcer, dropped Namath and Simpson and shifted Gifford to the analyst's chair. Ironically, it was this one year, during which ABC used a two-man booth, that put the program in its current predicament.

The problem was that Gifford provided virtually no analysis.

The next step was to bring in a first-rate analyst. So ABC hired rising star Dan Dierdorf away from CBS in 1987.

The problem now was: What do you do with Giff? ABC did the unthinkable: It kept him.

This created a Gifford problem and a Dierdorf problem.

The Gifford problem is that he doesn't have anything to say.

The Dierdorf problem is that he says too much.

It would've been preferable if ABC had kept Gifford in sort of the host role, setting up the game beforehand and rejoining the telecast at the half. Gifford, thus, would've been like the maître d' at a fine restaurant, greeting patrons as they came in and checking back with them later. But ABC went one step too far—it had Giff actually sit down with the customers and share the meal.

Giff has excellent table manners, but his being around just means smaller portions for everyone.

Dierdorf, meanwhile, has a sharper analytical eye. But Dierdorf never has seemed to realize he's in a three-man booth. (It might help if ABC put him in the middle, so that he could easily see announcers on either side.) Dierdorf obviously is frustrated—so much he wants to say, so little time to say it.

Among Dierdorf's frequent offenses is a penchant to jump on every referee's call, à la NBC's Bob Trumpy, and an insistence to follow the Repeat the Same Statement in Case Some People Didn't Get It the First Time Technique.

For instance, during a Bengals-Seahawks Monday night game, it appeared there might be a penalty called on the Bengals for running into a Seahawks punt returner on a fair catch.

Dierdorf, in semi-hysteria, said: "I don't know how you can call that. I don't know how you can call that. I don't know how you can call that. . . . Aw, come on, you can't call that. No way you can call that."

Well, as it turned out, they didn't call that.

He does this about ten times per game. I mean, he must do it about ten times per game.

Three-in-a-booth is a flawed concept. When Michaels, Tim McCarver and Jim Palmer did it in baseball, they talked too much, but at least they appeared to be pulling on the same oar. With Michaels, Dierdorf and Gifford, it's more like every time one guy climbs into the boat, someone else goes overboard.

The broadcast booth becomes a chatterbox. By the end of the night, you feel like you've watched two games instead of one. Between every play, Dierdorf weighs in for a while on a replay, then Gifford comes in briefly with some empty bromide, then by the time the ball is being snapped, Michaels barely has time to set the down and yardage.

All this talk leaves Michaels in an almost untenable position. Here is one of America's preeminent play-by-play broadcasters, and he's always weighed down by a three-man booth. Saddling Michaels with two jock analysts is like telling Michelangelo you're bringing in Earl Scheib and Sherwin-Williams to help him touch up the Sistine Chapel.

Michaels is the one who should set the tone on a telecast, he's the one who can set the story line best, he's the one who should be dominant. But on "Monday Night Football," he's the one being shut out.

This is very, very stupid.

The folks from ABC can come back in now.

Holy Toe-Loop!
How Does Skating
Figure to Be a Sport?

OK, already, with all this figure skating. The next time I see it on TV, regardless of my position on the couch, I will spring into the first triple-axel triple-flip triple-lutz triple-loop triple-salchow triple-twist double-toe-combination Chuck Norris-back spiral à la Van Damme.

That's right. I'm going to kick the damn set in.

Then I'm going to replace the mute button on my new remote with the anti-Dick Button.

Then I'm going to get me a beer, belly up to some steak 'n' fries and chant out, "No more NutraSweet."

I say: Hello, spring football; bye-bye, compulsory figures.

(Yes, folks, I am Neanderthal Man—*Homo neanderthalensis*—and like other Paleolithic guys, I prefer my caves cold and my weekends violent. Note the large, thick skull on my bookjacket photo. Until about 30,000 years ago, our family slogan was, "I came, I saw, I dragged your mother across the village square by her hair." My earliest ancestors had multiple divorces. I hate tax accountants.

The bottom line is this: If I'm pinned into my home, required to watch fifty-two weekends of TV sports a year because of some bad contract negotiated by my former lawyer, it had better be REAL SPORTS.)

Sports television in America these days is reduced to figure skating all winter and beach volleyball all summer. (Don't get me started on beach volleyball. These guys have perfect bodies, perfect hair, perfect tans and ridiculously large bank accounts, and chances are one of these fine fellows is even dating my ex-wife. Their major concern is to check the "high tide" chart in the paper every morning. And the next car I see with a LIFE IS A DAY AT THE BEACH bumper sticker better have darn good auto insurance.) Even in a non-Olympic year, figure skating dominates network television, with forty hours or so of coverage. To some of you, forty hours in a year may not seem like much—granted, many areas literally get forty TV hours of college basketball on any given Saturday in February—but this much weekend ice time for what is essentially a non-sport can be disturbing to Stone Age viewing intelligentsia such as myself.

In other words, someone has got to rescue me from Scott Hamilton.

For those of you still with me—I assume, at this point, we already have lost the namby-pamby letter writers and "thirtysomething" habitués—let's briefly review the most commonly confused athletic areas in terms of whether they are sports or not:

- Freestyle swimming, yes; synchronized swimming, no.

- Speed skating, yes; figure skating, no.

- Long-distance running, yes; gunrunning, no.

To be a sport, you must either have 1) a ball, 2) a race, or 3) a fight. This is really a rule without exception. The problem with such entities as figure skating and gymnastics is that judges always decide the winner, and this becomes both confusing and intensely political. With international panels, if a Bulgarian judge, say, had some bad coq au vin the night before, will he or she have a subconscious anti-French bias the next day?

Now, I can shout all I want about the lunacy of this figure skating craze, but I know those TV types will ignore me as usual because, frankly, figure skating does very well in the TV ratings.

In fact, drawing a lot of women who usually don't watch other sporting fare, figure skating clobbers the competition. Indeed, for many, figure skating offers grace and beauty and style and athleticism.

That's *entertainment,* but it's not necessarily sport.

Sure, these people are tremendous performers. Perhaps these performances, though, would be better appreciated *in private.* (For instance, I often pirouette through my living room wearing only a pink frock and a frilly tutu while singing "Tie a Yellow Ribbon 'Round the Old Oak Tree"—and it's quite a sight—but I'm not looking for TV coverage.)

I just wish the Duchesnays would throw more dinner parties and less skating fits.

Whatever figure skating is, ABC does it best. ABC's cameras seem to be in all the perfect spots, the cameras lead the skaters just right and the direction is near-flawless. Figure skating simply looks better on ABC, much the same way that, say, good perfume just smells better on Michelle Pfeiffer.

That's not to say that figure skating *sounds* better on ABC. It was ABC that first brought us the "postmodernist postskating interview" during the 1988 Winter Olympics, in which one David Santee would ask the same question of dozens of breathless skaters as they came off the ice: "How do you feel about your performance?" Santee has moved on—hopefully abroad—but the tradition continues in the hands of countless other probing interviewers.

Meanwhile, ABC's main analytical voices—Peggy Fleming and Dick Button—remain in place. Fleming has been with ABC since 1981 and Button since 1962.

What can be said of Fleming? She wears more shoulderless fashions on air than any other U.S. broadcaster and she occasionally speaks, sometimes extemporaneously.

Button—sometimes referred to as Bud Collins on skates or Dick Vitale with a beard—remains the excitable boy of rinks worldwide. He delights in stirring performances and chides others who skate without flair. He punctuates almost every move on ice. Still, most of his commentary can be reduced to the following expressions, depending on whether the skater completes a jump successfully or not:

"That was nice!" or . . . "Oh, no!"

"Wonderful height!" or . . . "Oh, no!"

"An elegant jump!" or . . . "Oh, no!"

"Good girl!" or . . . "Oh, no!"

Now, I haven't even touched upon pairs skating, or worse

than that, the so-called sport of . . . well, I don't even like to say it. Thankfully, I am out of time, so all I will say is this:

Ice fishing, yes; ice dancing, no, no, no, a thousand times no.

Weddings Are Nice, but I'm Married to Sports on the Tube

I had to go to a wedding the other Sunday. (The drug war, rightfully so, is garnering most of our attention these days, but this inexorable march toward matrimony among young, healthy couples is an oft-overlooked problem the nation also needs to confront.) Tip-off time for the ceremony was 12:30 P.M. ET, meaning the reception would be pitted head-to-head timewise with Game 7 of the NBA Eastern Conference finals on TV.

Now, I couldn't just bag the wedding; it was a close relative getting married—a cousin or something—and as a once-respected family member, I was expected to be at Table 19.

(Incidentally, I generally get placed no closer to the head table at these affairs than my books do to the front of bookstores.)

But to my way of thinking, this basketball match easily outdistanced this connubial match in importance. All the wedding would do is legally bind two people for, perhaps, four or five years before the union ended in unpleasant dissolution.

Meanwhile, this Game 7 would decide whether the Pistons or the Bulls—both eminently capable of beating the Western Conference champion Trail Blazers—would make it to the finals and likely bring home an NBA title that folks in Detroit or Chicago would cherish for a lifetime.

Clearly, this was not a game to miss, but it was going to be missed.

I had forgotten, though, that this is America. In America, life doesn't ever go on without a TV set nearby.

It's the curious thing about the way we are. Momentous events in any family's life cycle—holidays, births, confirmations, weddings, funerals—seem to be nothing more than nagging interruptions for many sports fans, who will always manage to find a way to watch that day's game of choice.

A few years back, I was at a wedding that had the misfortune of being in Washington, D.C., the day that the Redskins were in the NFC championship game. Within minutes after the reception began, a nine-inch TV set had been brought in—by one of the ushers—and plugged in at one of the tables in a corner of the room. Soon enough, there were twenty, maybe twenty-five people (almost all men) crowded around the table. I gravitated toward the women who were whining about the spectacle, playing the part of the liberated male; what they didn't know was that I was taping the game at home and trying to get through the afternoon without hearing a score.

So on this recent Sunday, I was not so much shocked as soothed when I thought I heard the familiar sounds of crowd noise in a sold-out arena. Suddenly, I realized that the game was near. As the band at the reception was striking up "We've Only Just Begun"—must we hear that at every wedding?—I struck out to find Michael Jordan on the premises.

Ah, the kitchen.

God bless the kitchen.

To the left of the sink, to the right of a colander, with a spatula sitting oddly on top of it as if some sort of antenna, there sat a television set. The cord barely stretched to the wall outlet, the picture was black-and-white with a ghost or two and Verne Lundquist's voice sometimes was drowned out by hot water splashing violently into some nearby pots, but, indeed, it was the Pistons and the Bulls, live, from hundreds and hundreds of miles away, through some remarkable, inexplicable technology called television.

To hell with those little wieners rolled up in bread, I was going to watch hoops.

So I watched, but I also winced.

The game needed no gaudy introduction, but this was Lundquist's: "The champions—the current holders of the crown. The challengers—the team intent on taking that title away. The Pistons and the Bulls . . . both focused on winning, both determined to take that final step. To repeat as champion, to become a champion, you must be relentless in your pursuit, unyielding in your desire, single-minded in your goal. For a champion will ultimately pay any price—*pay any price*—for success. In Game 7, you can hold nothing back or save anything until later, for after today, there may not be a tomorrow."

Whoa!

Yo, Verne, take a Valium and chill out a little.

Meanwhile, analyst/legal eagle Len Elmore had a horrendous day, setting the tone early by offering, "Certainly, every possession is going to be important in this game." In the late going, Elmore insisted, "This is a seventh game. You've got to lay everything out there." (The only thing worse than an ex-jock analyst is an ex-jock analyst with a law degree. Boy, can they talk. If Elmore's arguments were this weak when he was an assistant district attorney in Brooklyn, he couldn't have convicted a caterpillar of crawling.)

The game, unfortunately, became lopsided. (The wedding actually had more suspense when the best man momentarily couldn't locate the ring in his pocket.) When it ended, I returned to the reception hall. People were still celebrating the newly wed couple's good fortune. I didn't quite know what to do—there was no one I really wanted to talk to, and yet there was so much time to kill until the finals began two nights later.

Just Say No
to Baseball

I turned on the TV the other day. There was a baseball game on. Then I went out for a while, and when I got home, I turned on the TV again. There was a baseball game on. I got a little hungry, fixed myself a four-egg omelette, then took a nap. When I got up, I turned on the TV. There was a baseball game on.

Wherever you are right now in America, reach over and turn on the nearest TV, and there will be a baseball game on.

Once again, America is making an unscheduled mid-course correction in cultural direction, and the news is not particularly encouraging. Yes, baseball is a wonderful sport,

and yes, it's nice to have it served up as some sort of mean(
ing miniseries over the long, hot and lazy summer. But . .

The romance is gone.

Every time I look up, there's somebody else playing right
field.

Baseball has become the college basketball of the nineties.
The difference is that even with a basketball game—save for
select Big East contests—you know it will be over in two
hours. Baseball games can go on for two days. (There was a
thirteen-inning Cubs-Mets game in which New York catcher
Mackey Sasser, who had been at his father's funeral, got to Shea
Stadium shortly after midnight, prompting WWOR announcer
Ralph Kiner to explain, "If he plays, he'll have arrived tomorrow for today's game.")

The problem began in 1990, when baseball made a fundamental change: With ESPN on board, virtually every inning of
every game on every night of every week was beamed to some
television sets across the land.

And the problem was exacerbated when many baseball
fans made a fundamental mistake: We tried to watch it all.

Speaking for regular people* everywhere, I am here today
to say that we are wearier and wiser, and we no longer will try
to watch it all.

When you eat too much too fast at the dinner table, you get
sick to your stomach. Similarly, when you watch too much too
soon in the baseball season, you get sick to your scorecard.

Just Say No to Doug Drabek.

Baseball's regular season lasts 185 days or so. During that

---

*"Regular people" do not include Rotisserie League players, anyone ever
calling WFAN radio in New York, subscribers to *Baseball Digest, Baseball
America* or *Baseball Weekly,* Prime Ticket employees and their immediate
families, those who watched the exorcism last week on "20/20," lawyers or
Norm Hitzges.

time—via network TV, cable, superstations and over-the-air local broadcasts—there is an average of three TV games a day for six consecutive months.

That's a lot, frankly.

I believe it is time for a New Viewing Order to emerge, a rational, temperate and fair response to this glut of games, a reasonable, measured, judicious, logical and practical solution combining sporting needs, family obligations and sensible recreational management.

We're simply not going to watch anymore.

OK, OK, I'm not talking a full-scale boycott here, just a reduction in viewing force. The key is to pace ourselves. Nobody sprints at the beginning of a marathon. By Memorial Day last year, I had hit The Wall. I had nothing left for the long summer ahead, and even though I like John Saunders very much, I had to ask him to get out of my living room.

I have established guidelines to restrict my baseball-viewing hours:

- *No Seattle Mariners games.* I love Ken Griffey, Jr., I love the Pacific Northwest, I love 10–8 slugfests that end just before dawn in the East. But in The Big Picture—and I'm talking here about the entirety of birth and life and death and the afterlife—it is just incongruous that anyone spend more quality time with the Mariners than with, say, someone sleeping in the same bed. I felt like a partial-plan Mariners season-ticket holder last year. For my viewing purposes from here on in, the AL West is a six-team division and the Kingdome is an amusement park.

- *No Chris Berman.* This really is a simple, painless decision, like deciding not to ever touch any beets on your plate. Berman apparently has some type of following among inhabitants of various state-run institutions, habitués of suburban shopping mall video arcades and hitchhikers looking to get to Monterey by the weekend. His you-can-check-out-but-you-can-never-leave, Hotel California shtick plays like a tacky, one-note lounge act in a roadway Ramada Inn. It's time the ESPN monster went *back back back back back* to wherever he came from, but there are so few scheduled flights to Pluto.

- *No TBS.* I've had it with the Braves, I've had it with "Hotlanta," I've had it with the Tomahawk Chop, I've had it with Ted and Jane, I've had it with these backwood homer announcers rooting on the home boys. This ain't a superstation, it's Mayberry with an extension cord. If Atlanta really is the new cultural mecca of this nation, I have a feeling Canada's going to get awfully crowded real soon. Spare me Skip Caray; I'll watch the Weather Channel before I watch another Mark Lemke at-bat.

- *No Tim McCarver before the All-Star break.* A lot of people I respect still think the CBS/WWOR voice is the best in baseball; I happen to think he's a one-man wind tunnel. What happens is that his encyclopedic knowledge of the short hop and his unparalleled understanding of proper double play depth wears me out in the early season. I also always have this vision of him squatting with a catcher's mask on at all times while he's on the air.

One final guideline to restrict my baseball viewing: When I get up during the seventh-inning stretch—*if* I get up—I'll just walk right out of the room and won't come back.

I Wanted to
Take a Nap,
So I Turned On
the TV to Watch Golf

I shanked my tee shot badly on the finishing hole, leaving
it midway between a Kmart and a Taco Bell, about a
quarter-mile off the golf course. I needed to get up and down in
eight on the par-four hole in order to break 120 for the first time
since the Carter administration.

I took out a three-wood—although I'd normally play a
pitching wedge off a parking-lot lie—and as I tried to locate the
distant 18th green, I heard them.

"I think he's playing a three-wood," ABC's Steve Melnyk
said. "What have you got, Rossi?"

"It looks like a three-wood," ABC's Bob Rosburg said. "But
I can't tell if he's got a clear line back to the fairway. Judy?"

"He's got a decision to make, Rossi," ABC's Judy Rankin whispered. *"If he tries to play it with a right-to-left fade, he's got a problem with the Ford Bronco Ranger. And even if he tries to just lay it back in front of the creek, I think the Fotomat comes into play."*

"From my vantage point," ABC's Jerry Pate offered, *"his best bet is to shoot it low, carry under the interstate overpass and let it run down the exit ramp back onto the golf course."*

"I think that's the smart play, considering the crosswind and the No Stopping Anytime sign," ABC's Ed Sneed added.

I just left my ball there and quit the game altogether.

I'm of two opinions on golf: One, it shouldn't be played; two, it shouldn't be watched.

I am prepared to defend my position on both counts, and I promise not to speak any louder than Mark Rolfing.

(But first, let me briefly summarize my feelings regarding ESPN's new Pro Athletes Golf League—composed of current and former baseball, basketball, football and hockey players—and the burgeoning twenty-four-hour Golf Channel on cable:

No, no, no, a thousand times no.)

Golf dates to fifteenth-century Scotland. In its earliest days, greens fees were waived if you knew Mary, Queen of Scots. Golf evolved as a class-system divider—the haves created the divots, the have-nots replaced the divots. The game came to America as early as the seventeenth century; miniature golf—known as Putt-Putt—was popularized among lower-class masses who could only afford a single club, thus leaving longer, regular courses to the privileged gentry types.

Golf remains a game of the rich, for the rich and by the rich. I believe it was Jefferson who said, "Were it left to me to decide whether we should have a government without golf courses, or golf courses without government, I should not hesitate a moment to prefer the latter." (Baltusrol Golf Course clubhouse, Springfield, New Jersey, January 16, 1787.)

You hardly ever see anybody taking the bus to play golf.

Sure, there are more and more public courses, but golf remains a country club sport. Country clubs linger on as one of the few institutions in the nation in which discrimination against minorities not only is curiously standard but also is routinely expected by longtime members.

Aside from the sociocultural shortcomings of the game, golfers also invite scorn for one other reason—the way they dress.

Golfers dress as if Walt Disney threw up on them.

Incidentally, golf is wonderful exercise, particularly for the caddy carrying the clubs.

Let's talk TV golf, shall we? (But quietly, please: Somewhere nearby, some golfer probably is contemplating whether to use a putter on the fifteenth green or whether to just bump the ball in with his foot while no one is looking, and the slightest disturbance might knock him clear across the bunker. Someone has to explain to me how gymnasts can perform on the balance beam while the crowd is cheering on other gymnasts and music is blaring from floor-exercise routines but a professional golfer cannot address the ball unless there is dead silence in the entire tristate region.)

I must be honest right from the start on this TV discussion—the very pace of golf is really nap-inducing and Steve Melnyk's southern drawl is really nap-inducing and those azaleas and dogwoods are really nap-inducing and all that music on golf telecasts is really nap-inducing. So, in the interest of full disclosure, I must admit to readers at this point that any notes I took while watching golf on TV were compiled entirely while I was snoozing.

Yes, folks, golf arguably is the greatest thing for sleep since the invention of the coil-spring mattress.

Traditionally, the only golf tournaments worth watching on TV are the four Grand Slam events. Not that Mark McCumber doesn't turn me on. But in most of these other nickel-and-dime tournaments, everyone pretty much looks the same. (Speaking of which—and I hate to harp on this whole fashion business—but who exactly dresses these pro golfers in the morning? I haven't seen trousers like those since attending the National Direct Mailers Association convention in Stroudsburg, Pennsylvania, in 1967. You've seen one set of loud, checkered polyester pants, you've seen them all.)

Anyway, I'm not even going to discuss NBC, which televises the Jamie Farr Toledo Classic and about fifteen other Jamie Farr-like tournaments. Actually, when I've glanced at NBC golf—which has the astute Johnny Miller and a cast of castaways—it doesn't even look right. Trying to watch golf on NBC is like trying to eat soup with a fork.

That leaves CBS, home of the Masters, and ABC, home of a brigade of on-course reporters.

Advantage CBS.

Not only is the Masters by far the best tournament but it also benefits from CBS's bang-bang-bang approach to coverage—just shot after shot, tee to fairway to green, unadorned. CBS nearly manages to make golf look like an action sport. CBS just shows you the shots, without a lot of conjecture about club selection and crabgrass. And, if nothing else, it's always a pleasure watching Jack Nicklaus as he approaches the green at each of the closing holes, with that patented wave of the hand to acknowledge the appreciative gallery. (I did the same thing at my wedding, although it was misinterpreted by many as an attempt to make a pass at some of the bridesmaids.)

Meanwhile, the folks at ABC don't just cover golf, they smother it. For the U.S. Open, ABC is there for all eighteen holes with nearly thirty cameras. Plus, ABC hires this on-course army—Bob Rosburg, Judy Rankin, Ed Sneed and the like—to surround each hole. They're in the rough, they're behind the trees, they're part of the gallery. They're always lurking, like bad news. If a shot goes astray, they're TV golf's version of medics rushing to the scene to attend the wounded.

In addition, these on-course reporters insist on gauging the quality of each shot while it's in the air. This is abundantly unnecessary. First of all, viewers are going to see how the shot turns out in about two seconds. Second, about every other time Rosburg or Rankin or Sneed goes, "It's right at the flag, a good-looking shot," it's not.

Then again, what am I complaining about? I'm asleep by this point.

Forget March Madness—
I'm Numb by Late
November

A meteorite falls to Earth, unleashing an icky, sticky goo. The slime grows, gathering size and speed, sweeping away everything in its path. It is a parasite, a lethal lump of insatiably hungry goop, a slurping, slithering mass of ooze. It creeps and leaps and glides and slides, making its way into bars, hotel lounges and living rooms across the land. It is a piece of Jungian slime, attacking and destroying both willing and unwilling victims. It is a media monster.

It's The Blob, circa 1993.

It's televised college basketball.

My God, it's here already.

College basketball these days begins every mid-November and continues uninterrupted until early April. There are, oh, 1,200 televised college basketball games over a 140-day period.

That's right, 1,200 games. A few years ago, the TV count topped 1,000, and I said: Sell. I was wrong. Where there's a will, there's a way, and where there's a game being played, there's cable being laid.

Of course, I speak of ESPN.

Actually, ESPN does *only* 200 games or so annually, with the rest rounded up from networks and cable outlets, syndicators and the other usual broadcasting suspects.

I don't mind 1,200 basketball games on TV, it's just that the first 1,125 mean absolutely nothing. So I'm not exactly sure why, but each autumn I tune in to the Big Apple NIT, also known as the Preseason NIT. From all indications, there is no reason for these games to be either played, televised or viewed.

I mean, if you consider the college basketball campaign to be the sporting equivalent to the Hundred Years' War (1337–1453), then some Evansville-at-Oklahoma State game played one week into the season is really no more meaningful than the battles of Sluis (1340), Crécy (1346) and Calais (1347). Heck, the Hundred Years' War didn't even heat up until Henry V routed the French at Agincourt in 1415—a full 936 months into the conflict—so why would anybody get pumped up if Eddie Sutton gets a technical foul in late November of any year?

Eventually, though, the meaningless matches of December, January and February give way to this mania called March Madness. The first part of this postseason fest ESPN calls Championship Week. Over nine days, ESPN shows thirty-odd conference tournament games. It is particularly difficult to keep up with ESPN and the networks on the final weekend of this Championship Week, because so many games are going on at once. But I've been around the block—I literally take a 10-minute walk once a month to keep in shape—and I know the best way to deal with this mind-boggling oversaturation.

You need more than one TV. And you need good snacks.

Here are the best ways to make this conference tournament thing work on that final big day:

Plan A
(Have Couch, Won't Travel)

1:00–2:30 P.M.: Watch SEC and ACC tournaments.

2:30–2:45: Eat Budget Gourmet Linguini With Bay Shrimps & Clams Marinara entree.

2:45–3:45: Watch SEC, ACC and Metro games.

3:45–4:35: Call a friend on the phone who can describe Big West and Big East games that you can't see.

4:35: Order Pizza Movers' large pepperoni pizza.

4:35–6:10: Watch ACC and Big East games, dial-hopping to Indiana-Illinois contest in hopes of catching the occasional technical foul on either bench.

6:10–8:05: Watch Big West final.

8:05–8:10: Eat two Kit Kat bars.

8:15–9:55: Watch Midwestern Collegiate Conference final.

Total Calories: 1,650. Total Cost: $14.75 ($11.75 if pizza is not delivered within thirty minutes).

Plan B
("Darling, I'll Meet You by Lingerie in a Couple of Hours")

Noon: Talk with family members, falsely leading them to believe you have little interest in day's games.

12:30: Do a few bills with the ECAC North Atlantic final on sans sound, falsely leading them to believe you have little interest in day's games.

2:35: Offer to take family members shopping to local mall, falsely leading them to believe you have little interest in day's games. (Do NOT scan radio in the car, hoping to pick up some stray play-by-play.)

2:45: After arriving at mall, buy everyone an ice cream cone and tell family members they can shop freely for several hours, falsely leading them to believe you have little interest in day's games. Then immediately head for Sears' Audio/ Video Center, where you can watch six games at once in the TV section until late afternoon.

Total Calories: 125. Total Cost: $5.25 to $395.99, depending on sales.

Plan C
(ESPN or Bust)

8 A.M.: Take American Airlines or USAir flight to New York's La Guardia Airport, then hitch a ride to ESPN's Bristol, Connecticut, studios.

12:30 P.M.–midnight: After convincing ESPN honchos you are a die-hard fan who wants the most authentic viewing experience, sit in front of the dozens of monitors to watch every moment of every game, grabbing all the donuts, Doritos and coffee you can.

Midnight–4:55 A.M.: Ask Dick Vitale a question.

Total Calories: 6,780. Total Cost: $458 ($589 if you take a taxi from the airport).

Championship Week, of course, leads directly into the NCAA Tournament, televised by CBS exclusively all the way to the title game, by which time most of us will be found in one horror-filled lump of lifelessness.

A Survivor's Tale:
Twenty-four Hours of ESPN

Since 1985, I have proudly served my country as a licensed sports television critic.

I've interviewed Howard Cosell. I've watched three football games simultaneously. I've sat through Energizer bunny commercials. I've even read the parts of *USA Today*'s sports television column that contain complete sentences.

But I had yet to climb the highest viewing mountain. At *L'Academie des Sports Television Critics,* we were told that sooner or later, because ESPN was a twenty-four-hour-a-day sports network, each of us would have to watch ESPN for twenty-four consecutive hours. Why? Because it's there.

I finally got there over the weekend.

From Friday at 6 P.M. until Saturday at 6 P.M., ESPN and I were one. And you thought driving the "Twenty-four Hours of Le Mans" was a tough journey? Hah! At least those guys have a seat belt. Here are highlights of my "Twenty-four Hours of ESPN" adventure:

5:59 P.M. Friday: I spoon out a large dish of vanilla fudge ice cream as a preparatory meal.

6:02: Barry Tompkins opens U.S. Olympic Festival with the words, "So sit back, relax and don't go away." I'm not going anywhere, Barry.

7:15: Because of satellite problems, there is no audio during the second half of "SportsCenter." I try to lip-read anchor Chris Fowler briefly but determine it is unlikely the Yankees have been sold by George Steinbrenner to a Milwaukee brewery headed by Vincent Price and Spiro Agnew.

10:20: Gary Thorne and Norm Hitzges weigh in for two and a half hours from the Blue Jays–Angels baseball game. (Isn't this how they tortured the protagonist in *A Clockwork Orange?*)

12:45 A.M. Saturday: "SportsCenter" is co-anchored by Anne Montgomery and Larry Burnett, who is growing a beard.

2:01: I take in the Water Skiing Masters with John Sanders and Wayne Grimditch, generally acknowledged as the best outdoor water skiing announcer team in cable history.

2:06: If I put the television set inside of the microwave, would the 24 hours go by any faster?

2:08, 2:35, 3:09, 3:28, 8:01, 8:57, 10:04 and 10:56: I am enticed to call NOW to get my own "helmet phone," free with a paid subscription to *Sports Illustrated.*

2:25: After Andy Mapple's fine slalom run in the Water Skiing

Masters, Grimditch comments, "Well, Superman couldn't have done it any better."

3:31: Yes, it's the Kroger Classic from Kings Island, Ohio.

5:30: Just my luck—on "a special one-hour edition" of "Saturday Night Thunder," there's both IHRA Pro Bikes from St. Louis *and* the Barber Saab Pro Series from Lime Rock, Connecticut.

5:59: Reaching the midway point of my marathon, I celebrate with a Snickers bar, two Mallo Cups, two Scooter Pies, a box of PomPoms, three Necco wafers and a bottle of Yoo-Hoo.

7:00: The late-night "SportsCenter" is rebroadcast. Inexplicably, Burnett's beard appears to have grown from the time of the live telecast.

7:30: "ESPN Outdoors" begins its 3½-hour Saturday morning block. I never go outdoors, so it's nice to see it's still there.

7:35: My blood sugar level exceeds the Dow Jones Industrial Average.

7:41: On "Sportsman's Challenge," Doug Hannon's No. 1 "Big Bass Fact" is the following—"Big bass aren't smaller than small ones."

8:04: On "The Outdoorsman with Buck McNeely," high-tech radio transmitters are planted into the abdominal cavities of largemouth bass so biologists can track the fish. (This could be all the rage in singles bars.)

8:30: On "Ultimate Outdoor Experiences with Wayne Pearson," they just shoot and kill birds for the entire half hour, with background action music provided.

9:57: I do four push-ups.

11:00: It's the "Powertrax All-American Pulling Series"—tractor pulls. Red Man chewing tobacco baseball caps abound.

11:23: I call my ex-wife, who was the one who filed for divorce, and tell her she made the right decision.

11:30: On "GameDay," Jimmy Roberts, usually a solid field reporter, comes indoors with a studio performance worthy of Albert Brooks's weekend anchoring stint in *Broadcast News*.

12:01 P.M.: It's the "Budweiser Thunder on the Ohio"—unlimited hydroplane racing. I am numb.

1:02: Play is canceled at the Kroger Classic. That means I must watch taped golf again, for two hours.

1:46: I want to commit telecide.

3:00: It's the pro bowlers' Miller Lite Challenge, sponsored by Budweiser. One, this confuses me, having one beer sponsor another beer's bowling event. Two, this disturbs me, being a Rolling Rock guy.

4:51: Calling the Miller Lite Challenge are Denny Schreiner and Mike Durbin, generally acknowledged as the best indoor bowling announcer team in cable history.

4:58: To ensure that I don't fall asleep, I have stopped blinking.

5:05: My main man Bart Conner is calling the women's gymnastics at the U.S. Olympic Festival. (You really haven't climbed the 24-hour viewing mountain until you've heard Bart Conner.)

6:00: I came, I saw, I conquered cable! There's another hour left in the Olympic Festival telecast, but I've gone the full 24 and decide to pass on it. Hey, I'm not crazy.

Born to Watch TV:
It's in the Genes

For years, I have lived with the guilt. While friends attended lavish dinner parties, I watched "Lifestyles of the Rich and Famous." While relatives gathered for birthday celebrations, I watched "Family Affair." While colleagues routinely got promoted, I watched "Who's the Boss?"

Let's face it: We never can watch as much television as we would like. (Actually, I just increased my viewing capabilities by constructing a TV stand—like the ones you see hanging over bars—that peers down over my bathtub. And I hooked up a unique wireless remote, with the hot-water tap controlling VHF stations and the cold-water tap for UHF channel-switching. The system is not cable-ready, though, and I haven't figured out a way to keep my glasses from steaming up as I shower.)

I've been through three therapists, one wife and four VCRs asking myself the $64,000 question: Why do I watch so much TV?

Now I finally know—it's not my fault.

The headline the other day leapt off the page and into my heart: SOME CHILDREN MAY BE BORN TV WATCHERS.

And there it was, a newspaper report—well, actually, not so much a newspaper report as one in *USA Today*—stating that according to a new study, TV-watching is genetically linked.

The study was conducted by Penn State psychologist Robert Plomin. He examined viewing habits of 459 families—half of which had adopted kids—and determined that family environment accounts for only 20 percent of kids' viewing differences, "nonshared environment" (such as habits of friends) accounts for 35 percent and genetics 45 percent.

Thus, I'm not to blame for my television excesses. (My legal people will be contacting my parents ASAP. We hope to settle out of court, but I'm not averse to taking it to Judge Wapner.)

I was going to call Plomin over the weekend to question him on his findings, but I didn't want to miss "Columbo Goes to College."

Yes, I'm not responsible. I simply can't help myself. I have no choice but to watch and watch and watch.

I watched the NBA on TNT. I watched Ernie Johnson, Jr., in the studio. (Just a thought: If you put a lab jacket on Johnson, couldn't he pass for a pharmacist selling aspirin?) I watched Hubie Brown analyze the Celtics-Mavericks game and learned to use the expressions "shot opportunities," "attack the rim" and "break you down off the dribble."

I watched rodeo on ESPN. I watched these cowboys wrestle steers to the ground—it was reminiscent of men stalking women in many singles bars, only less direct—and I watched team roping.

I watched "NBA Inside Stuff" on NBC. (Only sixteen slam dunks during "Jam Session," a season low.)

I watched the NCAA Division III football title game on ESPN between Lycoming and Allegheny. I watched Bradenton, Florida's Southeast High School Band perform at halftime. (I hate to criticize high school kids—I really do—but the only thing that could've saved this band was a xylophone or Xavier Cugat.)

I watched Army-Navy on CBS. (The word "tradition" was used 2,683 times.) I watched Mike Francesa begin a pregame report, appropriately for him, at breakfast. I heard Tim Brant say after Navy used a shuffle pass, "It's usually a positive-yardage-gain type of play."

I watched two—two!!—triathlons. There was the taped "Escape From Alcatraz" on NBC and the taped "Ironman Triathlon" on ABC. Both networks used three announcers. (I hate three-in-the-booth on triathlons. Always have.) To provide us historical tidbits, NBC's Fred Roggin kept wandering Alcatraz and, remarkably, someone let him back out. Meanwhile, on ABC, the Ironman production—Sam Posey's baby—was better. Posey has that triathlon touch—the voice, the attitude, the eyebrows.

They swam, they ran, they cycled. I just watched.

I watched two—two!!—golf tournaments on ESPN. There was the Sazale Classic and there was the Kaanapali Classic. The latter was in Maui, and broadcasters Jim Kelly and Bob Murphy adhered to the time-honored You-Must-Wear-a-Hawaiian-Shirt-When-You're-Broadcasting-from-Hawaii Rule.

I watched "Body by Jake" four straight times.

I watched Chris Berman put on a "HelmetCam" during a ridiculous Beer Bowl commercial and I watched CBS use a "MuleCam" by mounting a cameraman onto Mike Fran— uh, excuse me, onto the Army mascot.

I watched the Michigan-Duke college basketball game. I also watched Arizona-LSU, Kansas-Kentucky, De Paul–Illinois State and Arkansas-Missouri. I will watch every college basketball game—all 1,240 of 'em—through the Final Four.

I watched the "Bowling Shootout" on NBC. I watched as $125,000 was on the line in the final frame. I watched Brian Voss get a strike. I then watched Lisa Wagner throw a strike ball, but the 7 pin wouldn't go down. It teetered. It shook. It wavered. It moved. But it wouldn't go down, and Voss won the money. It was the greatest "Bowling Shootout" I have ever seen, and I HAVE SEEN THEM ALL.

The phone rang. The doorbell rang. The alarm rang. I just kept watching.

I watched all the NFL pregame shows (except, of course, CNN's Snake Stabler thing). I watched Chris Berman on ESPN and was confused as to when he was hosting an NFL studio show and as to when he was hosting a Beer Bowl studio show.

I watched every NFL game allowed by law. I even tried to watch other NFL games in which I needed to pirate the signal, but I dropped my ball-peen hammer while trying to rewire some lines atop the telephone pole.

I watched "Chipmunks Rockin' Through the Decades" on NBC.

I watched and watched and watched, and one day the children of my children's children will have no choice but to watch, too. I hope they get better reception.

Is That a Tornado in the Distance? No, It's Chris Berman.

On a 19-inch TV screen, Chris Berman is an eight-hundred-pound gorilla. He rips and roars, zigs and zags, rumbles and stumbles and rambles and scrambles through scores and highlights. There's no letup, no pause, no give, no mercy. He pillages the senses. He's the Bay of Pigs. He's the Johnstown flood. He's the human train derailment.

He might be the single biggest detriment to athletics since the advent of jock itch.

Unfortunately, Chris Berman also might be the single biggest influence in sports television since Howard Cosell.

Berman's longstanding run in respectable circles prompts some simple questions:

Where did he come from? (Brown University. I guess some Ivy League schools have a fence through which you can sneak onto campus somewhere near the chemistry lab.)

Is society responsible for creating a guy like this? (Yes.)

And who exactly in Berman's entourage is saying, "Chris, *you're killing me with this stuff.* You're beautiful, babe!!"? (I don't know, but whoever it is should be ferreted out, frisked, gagged, stuffed and mounted.)

I would rather stand on my head in a vat of balsamic vinegar than watch Chris Berman.

I would rather buy a condo on Three Mile Island than watch Chris Berman.

I would rather stick my head in a car with twelve rabid weasels than watch Chris Berman.

I would rather listen to Tony Orlando at dawn than Chris Berman at dusk.

Berman is the lead player on an ESPN stage that often reduces sports to statistics, sound bites and snapshots. He is symptomatic of TV's Sno-Kone coverage of sports: We get served up some oversweetened syrup that we suck in mindlessly, then all that's left a couple of minutes later is some melting ice.

For years, ESPN's signature program, the thrice-daily "SportsCenter," has been overpopulated by a bunch of anchors who seemed like overgrown fans made good. The mix has gotten better in recent years—with thoughtful and clever voices such as Bob Ley, Charley Steiner and Keith Olbermann—but the flagship member of the frat pack remains Berman.

Berman owns Sundays at ESPN; all summer he anchors "Baseball Tonight" and all autumn he anchors "NFL Game-Day" and "NFL PrimeTime." (In Woody Allen's *Broadway Danny Rose,* Danny quotes his Aunt Rose as saying, "You can't ride two horses with one behind." Aunt Rose never met Chris Berman.) These shows are hour-long torture chambers. Berman's the lounge act from hell—full of lingo and slang and clichés and, of course, his trademark nicknames. Like pet rocks, the nicknames were a funny-for-a-moment fad that should have come and gone. When he delivers a nickname, he has nowhere to go; he's like a bodybuilder—he just poses, and then there's nothing else.

He's a one-dimensional force with little flair: Issues baffle him, players dazzle him. He'd be overmatched interviewing his own shadow.

So week after week, he enters your living room like the uncle every kid dreads, the one who pinches your cheeks and tells the same corny jokes. And week after week, more TV outlets decide they want more Bermans. His carousel style of sportscasting is the most imitated in the business today. (CNN's irritant savant, Van Earl Wright, is in many ways nothing more than a Chris Berman knockoff.)

At least Cosell had substance behind the shtick. Berman, meanwhile, is all mouth and no mind. He lacks perspective. He knows loads of meaningless trivia but possesses little meaningful knowledge. He's an apologist for players he sucks up to. He's the ultimate fan, thrilled to be on a first-name basis with big-time jocks.

He's a moon-faced phony with a national forum. And what a forum it is: He gets his own microphone, and he's on a cable network that operates twenty-four hours a day, 365 days a year. (Like 7-Eleven, ESPN never even closes to clean up the place a bit.) One day, ESPN may even spin off Berman and create an all–Chris Berman network.

In fact, ESPN keeps bloating Berman's presence. Since 1990, Berman has attempted baseball play-by-play, sort of like Axl Rose doing *Aida*. But he doesn't so much do play-by-play as provide a running monologue with the game as a backdrop. Often, Berman is not even paying attention to the action on the field; it ends up sounding like the old slide-projector presentation in junior high, when the accompanying narration on the record player is always one slide off from what you're actually seeing.

In 1992, I actually stayed with ESPN and Berman for nearly the entirety of a fourteen-inning Orioles-Royals game that lasted four hours and twenty-one minutes. It was like watching a toilet overflow.

Sure, I know that old expression, "Into each life a little rain must fall." Yeah, well, I'm standing here port side on Noah's ark and it's pouring buckets of Chris Berman and there's not an umbrella strong enough to withstand this deluge. When will it ever let up?

Coming Soon
to a TV Set
Near You . . .

Sports rights fees have gotten expensive. (It costs more to telecast the Summer Olympics, for instance, than to invade a Persian Gulf nation.) So broadcast and cable networks are looking for new, cheaper ways to present sports programming. They have stumbled upon two solutions:

(1) Rebroadcast great events of the past.
(2) Create new events in which costs can be controlled, like filming an entire program out of a linen closet.

As for the second solution, I have sources—yeah, people *do* talk to me—who have provided the following list of upcoming network and cable sports offerings currently in development. (Note: Program descriptions are provided by the broadcast and cable networks themselves.)

- "The Bob Hope Nudist Desert Colony Classic" (NBC): Leading figures from both the sporting and entertainment worlds play ninety holes of golf in the buff. Charlie Jones, wearing only a headset, anchors.

- "Return of The American Sportsman" (ABC): In a twist on the longtime series, Kodiak bears and Tasmanian wolves try to hunt down Curt Gowdy and a guest celebrity.

- "Wide World of Notre Dame" (NBC): Spanning South Bend, Indiana, to bring us the constant variety of sport and big business—the thrill of alumni and the agony of paying taxes—the network will include first-time live coverage of the annual spring football scrimmage and point-of-view cameras following Fighting Irish student-athletes on their way to the campus library.

- "Masterpiece Basketball" (PBS): The game's elder statesman, Alistair McGuire, chronicles the evolution of the entry pass.

- "The Best of Bart Conner" (ABC): The talented gymnast/broadcaster/raconteur sings selections from Verdi's *La Traviata* while straddling the pommel horse on figure skates.

- "This Week in Strat-o-Matic Baseball" (Prime Ticket): An inside look at the popular board game, with regular segments on dice management.

- "This Week in Rotisserie League Baseball" (Prime Ticket): An inside look at the popular fantasy game, with regular segments on how to dress like a geek with no life.

- "Tour de SportsChannel" (NBC): A scaled-down version of the defunct Tour de Trump, with the network passing on production costs of its de facto, near-defunct cable programming arm, SportsChannel America. The cycling stages will be rerouted to include only those areas in which SportsChannel America has a regional affiliate.

- "Tour de Trumpy" (NBC): Popular NFL analyst Bob Trumpy guides viewers through a different room of his Cincinnati home each week, with occasional stopovers at the VCR to sample some of his best boxing and golf play-by-play work.

- "Tour de Oh My God, There's Been an Accident" (NBC): A bicycle race through New York City, featuring deliverymen and messengers balancing produce, documents and pizzas on their handlebars while dodging in and out of rush-hour traffic and avoiding the taunts and honks of Manhattan's legendary cabdrivers.

- "Greatest Moments in Arena Football" (ESPN): Each week, one moment will be highlighted from the sport's brief but storied history. The show will be preempted those weeks in which a greatest moment cannot be found.

- "The Bob Love Boat" (WGN): The former Chicago Bull great is joined by other ex-Bulls on a bizarre cruise ship sailing Lake Michigan. With Tom Boerwinkle as recreation director, Norm Van Lier as bartender and Jerry Sloan as The Skipper.

- "Bowling for Internships" (syndicated): Students from top national universities compete for summer jobs on Capitol Hill.

- "Lifestyles of America's Most Wanted" (Fox): Hosted by a rotating panel of NBA, NHL and NFL players currently on league suspension, this hybrid concept will feature high-resolution helicopter shots over south Philadelphia and San Quentin.

- "Jane Fonda Workout Video VIII" (TNT): America's leading workout beauty joins Ernie Johnson, Jr., and Pete Van Wieren in introducing an exercise regimen geared toward men who just don't like getting up from the couch. Colorized.

- "Peter Fonda Workout Video I" (TNT): America's leading good-for-nothing brother introduces a controversial exercise regimen in which the erstwhile actor demonstrates how to wake up about noon, ride a Harley over to 7-Eleven to buy two packs of cigarettes and a cup of coffee, stop by Sis's house to hit her up for a loan and get back to the apartment in time to watch "People's Court."

- "The Life and Times of Ahmad Rashad" (NBC): Based on the *The Life and Times of Grizzly Adams,* it's the story of a man accused of a downfield clipping penalty he has not committed who then seeks refuge as a network sportscaster and discovers that life there suits him better than life at a car dealership. Starring Ahmad Rashad as himself and Michael J. Fox as Bob Costas.

- "Paddock Point of View" (Prime Ticket): Live from Santa Anita, Pimlico and Aqueduct, a panel of horses rates the top jockeys and handicaps the day's top races.

- "The Isuzu Marv Albert Challenge" (NBC): Five aspiring sportscasters participate in three events—a Marv Albert sound-alike competition, a Marv Albert look-alike contest and a guess-Marv-Albert's-actual-age lottery. Winner spends a day of quality time in Buffalo with Paul Maguire. Cohosted by Steve Albert and Al Albert.

- "Chris Berman at Disney World" (ESPN): In a special "Outside the Lines" presentation, the two-time national sportscaster of the year roams the Orlando grounds in search of his next generation of viewers.

- "On the Road . . . With John Madden" (CBS): The popular sportscaster, using the CBS Chalkboard, details alternatives to overcrowded interstate highways.

- "In the Yard . . . With John Madden" (CBS): The popular sportscaster, using the CBS Chalkboard, details the best methods of effectively dealing with crabgrass.

- "At the Market . . . With John Madden" (CBS): The popular sportscaster, using the CBS Chalkboard, details crafty ways in which to butt in line at express lanes.

- "Kate & Al" (Fox): Susan Saint James (wife of NBC Sports president Dick Ebersol) reprises her Emmy Award-winning CBS sitcom role, joined by a new roommate—The Coach, Al McGuire. In the series premiere, Kate teaches Al how to book a super-savers airline fare and Al tries to explain the breakaway-foul rule (two shots plus possession) to Kate.

- "The USFL: An Oral History" (NFL Films): This 10-minute special captures highlights of the league's three-year history, including rare footage of a Needham, Massachusetts, man renewing his season tickets to the Boston Breakers.

- "The WLAF: An Oral History" (NFL Films): Dick Vermeil talks for a half hour.

- "Wide World of Frank and Kathie Lee" (ABC): This 90-minute special, shot on location in Vail, Colorado, follows the Giffords on their monthly shop-ski-and-stump trip. Cohosted by Regis and Cody. An Aaron Spelling production.

- "It Was a Lock" (Prime Ticket): Leading ex-bookies recount horror stories from the world of professional gambling, including a weekly "The Bet That Broke Me" segment detailing the one game that tapped out the player, destroyed his marriage and retired him to church bingo.

- "Body by Jake LaMotta" (ESPN): Fast-food tips from the ex–boxing great.

- "Battle of the Bulge" (TBS): Hulk Hogan, Randy Savage and other leading professional wrestlers reenact major Revolutionary War and Civil War combat scenes, demonstrating how history would have been altered if each battle's winner had been predetermined.

- "The Shirts and Skins Game" (NBC): NBA Eastern and Western Conference all-stars participate in an old-fashioned schoolyard hoops contest, with each team required to have two players on court at all times carrying a set of golf clubs.

- "Sports Illustrated: The TV Series" (HBO): Tastefully clad models read selected stories from each week's issue, plus a behind-the-scenes look at how the magazine's editors decide what necktie to wear to the office every day.

- "Meet the Zone Press" (C-SPAN): Moderated by Fred Barakat, a panel of coaches discuss the finer points of clock management, debate the intricacies of double-team pressure in the backcourt and examine tax breaks on the purchase of blackboards, chalk and towel racks.

- "Earlier . . . with Bob Costas" (NBC): This noontime treat features highlights from the diminutive sportscaster's formative professional days as the play-by-play man for the ABA's Spirits of St. Louis.

- "The Jock Reporters" (ESPN): Cohosted by Ahmad Rashad and Peggy Fleming, America's top ex-jock sports journalists discuss the issues of the day, including play-by-play broadcasters who get in their way, bad speaking engagements and maniacal sports TV critics. Regular panelists include Bob Trumpy, Tim McCarver and Dan Dierdorf.

- The Pat O'Brien project (CBS): An as-yet-untitled series in development in which the hip and cool sportscaster acts in a hip and cool manner.

- "Toro! Toro! Stella D'Oro!" (Nickelodeon): An action-filled hour featuring bullfighting's brash and innovative matador, Cal O'Hara, who forgoes the traditional red cape in favor of taunting bulls with packaged breakfast treats.

- "Mike Francesa Is Hamlet" (CBS): An all-new "Hallmark Hall of Fame" production costarring Andrea Joyce as Queen Gertrude, with a special guest appearance by Dick Vitale as the Polonius from Hell. "This above all, to thine own self be true, *bayyybeeeeeeee!* Rosencrantz and Guildenstern, you've got *to get a T.O., bayyy-beeeeeeeee!*"

- "A Moment with Rudy Martzke" (cable public access): In a quarterly series of 30-second spots, the engaging and exhilarating *USA Today* sports television writer shares everything he has learned about life—most of it from NFL director of broadcasting Val Pinchbeck—over the previous three months.

- "The NutraSweet Challenge of Champions" (ABC): Top athletes taste-test twelve food and beverage items for artificial sweetener.

- "The Dream League" (ESPN): Hosted by the mercurial John Naber, two four-person squads wearing NFL team colors—each led by a celebrity ex-athlete—compete in sports trivia. The first to "gain one hundred yards"—as marked off on a football-field scoreboard by attractive female "Dream Leaguers"—gets a chance to perform physical feats (like hitting a softball) to score more points. Oh, wait a minute, this *is* a show already.

They Called It
a No-Fault Divorce,
but I Blamed ESPN

On Saturday, for the first time in thirty-eight baseball seasons, there was no "Game of the Week" on network television. I immediately called my ex-wife.

"Can you believe it?" I exclaimed. "With this new CBS baseball contract, there isn't a game on every Saturday. It's unbelievable. CBS is doing only sixteen regular-season games."

"I'm excited for you," she said, sounding mildly uninterested.

"You're missing the point," I charged on. "Since there's no baseball on this afternoon, I was thinking we might want to reconcile."

"Reconcile what?"

"Reconcile our relationship. Reconciliation, babe. You and me, together again. Let's bring the magic back to the marriage. Just like the old days—you wash, I dry . . ."

"You watch TV, I die watching."

"No, no. It'll be different this time. What do you say?"

There was a pause. Our future was hanging on this phone line.

"What about Brent?" she queried.

"Brent's gone."

There was another pause.

"OK," she said softly. "Let's go for it. I'll be over at about one."

"Great, that's just great," I bubbled. "I'll go buy us some— oh, geez, I completely forgot. The NBA playoffs begin today on the network."

"Isn't it just the first round?"

"Yeah, but it's the Knicks and the Celtics."

"All right, I'll slide by at about three or three-thirty."

"It's a doubleheader, honeybunch. Indiana-Detroit at three-thirty."

"I guess it won't hurt me to watch that with you," she offered.

"Well, the thing of it is, ABC's got the 'Firestone Tournament of Champions' on at the same time. You know how I am about bowling. I'll have two TVs out, so I wouldn't be very good company."

"I'll come by in early evening."

"The NBA playoffs are on TNT."

"TNT? Doesn't Turner do terrible basketball production?"

"It's the last couple of days of National Cable Month. I'm just trying to do my part."

"I'll come by at ten."

"Hearns-Olajide on Showtime."

"I'll come by at eleven-thirty."

" 'SportsCenter' on ESPN."

I thought I heard a click. It sounded suspiciously like my ex-wife had hung up on me, a fact confirmed a few moments later when I heard a dial tone in the middle of telling her where we would go after midnight.

I had lost her again. Hell, I'd lost her more often than NBC loses audio. But I gathered my thoughts, clutched the clicker and, tormented by this latest personal failure, did what I do best: I watched TV for a long, long time. It's what I do. It's who I am. It's why I go alone.

I made my way through the Saturday fare.

I listened for a while to Tommy Heinsohn on the Pacers-Pistons game. Every time Heinsohn spoke, though, my air-conditioning would shut off, an inexplicable phenomenon that forced me to turn exclusively to ABC.

On ABC, bowling analyst Nelson "Bo" Burton, Jr., told Chris Schenkel during the fifth frame of an early game, "That's about the most unusual seven-ten split that I've ever seen." (When Bo says that, you take notice, because here is a man who has seen more 7-10 splits than Raymond Burr has seen courtrooms.)

The night fare was as expected. The Hearns-Olajide fight was called by Steve Albert and Ferdie Pacheco, and The Fight Doctor offered his usual prescription to induce a headache— shrill, unending overanalysis. Then I watched "SportsCenter" on ESPN, and it looked like every other "SportsCenter" I've ever seen, and, heck, I must've seen 10,000 of them by now.

On Sunday, the phone jolted me out of a peaceful slumber a few minutes after noon. Who could be calling so ridiculously early? It was my ex-wife.

"I'm willing to give you another shot," she said, "and I'm

85 ■

going to be realistic and reasonable. How does your schedule shape up today?"

"I've got an NBA doubleheader at one, boxing at three, USF&G Golf at four."

"USF&G golf?!?!" she replied, sounding mildly unrealistic and unreasonable.

"Hey, USF&G is a major insurance company, for crying out loud. It's not like I'm watching some Mickey Mouse auto race on ESPN sponsored by an underwear manufacturer. I didn't watch any golf yesterday; this is the final round. Plus, Bryant Gumbel's announcing it on NBC."

"Bryant Gumbel does golf?"

"You know, midlife crisis and everything."

Then there was a long silence on the line.

"Norman," she said finally, "it's last-chance time for us. I want to make this work. I'll be over, then, at eight o'clock or so."

I began to weep.

"As God is my witness," I stammered, "ESPN now has a baseball game of the week every Sunday evening. The Cubs are at the Dodgers tonight."

"The choice is yours," she said. "You can either be an ex–cable home or I can be your ex-wife."

I thought about it a few seconds, but before I could speak she whispered sadly, "Call me if there's a rainout," and hung up. She well knows that it never rains in Los Angeles.

Hockey Is Loathsome, Especially on Ice

The Stanley Cup playoffs will be starting in just a matter of hours, and for those casual observers who lost interest in the National Hockey League season sometime before the All-Star break, this is all you need to know: Many of the teams playing for this prestigious championship lost more games than they won during the current regular season, which, as it were, began several years ago.

(To reduce potential reader violence, I'm going to ask all hockey fans to please remove themselves from the immediate vicinity of this chapter right now. For those of you unsure if you're a hockey fan, here's a simple test—if there are any words in this sentence you cannot understand, then you should excuse yourself at this point.)

About those hockey fans—it's not exactly a Wimbledon-type crowd, eh?

Hockey fans—Motto: Don't think and drive—drink so much beer, the NHL needs two intermissions to accommodate the long lines at the rest rooms.

Yes, I hate hockey.

The game gets a good flow going for thirty or forty seconds, and then—boom!!!—the gloves are off and there's a brief two-hour skirmish. This makes for a very herky-jerky entertainment presentation.

Imagine, if you will, if every time I started to express a profound and prophetic thought—*excuse me for a moment, I want to go beat up that* USA Today *TV pinhead who keeps writing about overnight ratings and schlockmeister agents*—I was interrupted because of the need—*Hey, you! Yeah, you! You call yourself an editor? Bring your pica ruler over here and I'll edit you a new face!!!*—to bash somebody over the head.

Now, dutiful readers may recall my diatribe against figure skating a few chapters back. Many letter writers/amateur shrinks probably interpreted that as some type of misplaced macho urge and lamented my Neanderthal, chauvinistic emotional tendencies.

But if objective onlookers consider the fact that I also loathe hockey, they should spot a trend here: I have this unquestionable disdain for ice and ice skates, which likely emanates from childhood experience.

Quick anecdote: I was seven, maybe eight years old, and my father decided to take my six brothers and me ice fishing at a nearby lake. It was January or February—very, very cold, 10 degrees tops, could've even been below zero—and we all bundled up in the late morning to fish. Actually, it might've been early afternoon. It was a Thursday or a Friday, I'm not sure. We drove over there—in a Ford Galaxie 500 or a Dodge Dart, if I recall correctly—and I remember I wasn't too crazy about all this because I had the flu or smallpox or maybe it was just a cold or the sniffles. So we drilled a hole in the ice with my father's Black & Decker, and we began fishing. Either my brother Steve or my brother Seve started to cry, because they weren't real men. My father slapped them across the face—or I think he just might've cut them, nothing serious, with a bait knife across the cheek—and that shut them up good. Finally, my brother Stan had a big bite, and he's fighting this baby for a good forty-five minutes, maybe an hour, and we know it's either a largemouth minnow or a Maryland humpback whale, and then, suddenly, he's pulled into the water by the thing. So my father tells my brother Stu to go in after him, and he does—and he disappears. Then Sam takes a shot, then Sinbad, then Steve and Seve. One by one, each dives in. My father yells at me to go next, but I refuse—partly because I don't swim, partly because I'm not stupid. We lost all six of my brothers, and the fish. It was terrifying, and to this day I don't like to get near any ice. Come to think of it, I had seven brothers, but Hunter didn't come with us that day. I haven't seen Hunter in a long time—he lives in Montana or Montego Bay—but the point is, ice sports scare me, or at least bother me a bunch.

Now, the one thing I do like about hockey is the concept of the penalty box. This circumvents the entire unwieldy judicial system—no arrest, no arraignment, no trial, no appeals—just a referee who's instant judge-and-jury and—bang!!!—you're guilty as charged. Of course, considering the severity of the crimes committed, the punishments are paltry. But the open-air penalty box is a step in the right direction and consistent with the call for public executions in this country; one day, we'll just have a firing squad between periods take care of a defenseman who has slashed a guy's ear off. ("Rangers penalty on No. 26, Joey Kocur, game misconduct and last cigarette for dismemberment, at 13:49.")

As for hockey on TV, who are we kidding? ESPN does a swell enough job—for years, the NHL was presented on something called SportsChannel America, which was available in close to fifty homes across the continent—but no matter how well hockey is televised, it's difficult to watch the game on TV.

You can't see the puck.

No matter how you dress it up, in live, full-speed action, the puck looks like a runaway bread crumb across a 19-inch TV screen.

And have you noticed how often the puck goes into the stands at 140 mph? At baseball games, fans bring gloves to catch foul balls. At hockey games, folks—with no gloves, no pads, no shin guards, no mouthpieces—still try to get in the way of the puck. That's all you need to know about hockey fans.

And, boy, I'm really excited that the NHL decided to expand its regular season from eighty games recently. (I didn't think you could expand on a season that never ends.) Maybe the National Weather Service can extend winter by an additional forty-five days to accommodate this scheduling change.

Yes, I hate hockey.

Now, air hockey, *that's* OK. Lots of scoring. Big puck. No fighting. No skates. No ice.

Made-for-TV
in the Good Old USA:
The NFL

It was the first autumn Sunday—crisp air, sharp smells, an endless blue sky—but more important, it was a football Sunday. In the cycle of changing seasons, none sweeps in with more force than the NFL on TV.

Baseball is a wonderful day-in-and-day-out companion for six months, but football is a weekly ritual the rest of the year. Television makes it so.

When you grow up with baseball, you look forward to the occasional outing to the ballpark with your father or friends. When you grow up with football, you look forward to watching every hometown game every Sunday on TV. The NFL brings the stadium to you.

This is the simple and amazing thing about the NFL's ever-lasting popularity: Millions upon millions grow up to follow the league more closely and completely than any other sport, without ever going to a game. Millions upon millions see their favorite team play every week, without ever giving thought of going to a game. Millions upon millions build their Sundays around the game on TV, without ever planning the rest of their real lives so diligently.

I grew up in Washington, D.C., where my buddies and I had an unspoken, never-broken Sunday agreement—we might play touch football, we might hang out at the plaza, we might just sit outside and shoot the breeze, but at precisely 12:30 P.M. ET, we'd each retreat indoors, turn on "The NFL Today" and settle in for six or so hours of the NFL. Granted, not everyone watched every NFL doubleheader, but no one—no one we knew or wanted to know, anyway—skipped the Redskins game.

"Monday Night Football" became a terrific exclamation point to the NFL weekend, but nothing compared with the viewing expectations with which I awakened every Sunday morning. The Redskins usually started at 1 P.M., but as they got better and played in bigger games that were nationally televised, many of their games did not begin until 4 P.M. On those occasions, by 3:58 I'd be bloated with anticipation. At kickoff, I'd often find the couch too distant and climb down closer to the TV.

I remember once, in ninth grade, the phone rang about five minutes into a critical Redskins-Cowboys game and my mother said it was for me. It had to be a mistake, I told her, nobody would call me at this hour. But indeed, it was a classmate, Cindy Jordan, whom confidantes had told me was "interested" in me (at fourteen, with all the social prowess of a fire hydrant, you don't take this information lightly). Cindy wanted to know if I wanted to come by later to work on a history project we'd been assigned together. I told her the Redskins game was on and I couldn't think about it at the moment, and I hung up. We never dated.

There were those, obviously, who went to the games—RFK Stadium sold out every week—and talked about the raucous, electric atmosphere. And, indeed, the games on TV would lose their appeal without the crowd on hand to generate the emotion and excitement. But on the occasions I was offered tickets, I'd turn them down, regardless of how good the seats were.

In a lifetime of living in Washington, I've been to RFK for an NFL game one time.

When I went, I missed the replays. I missed the graphics. I missed being on the 50-yard line for every play. I missed my kitchen and my bathroom. Technically, football is not the best TV sport. In basketball, for instance, one mid-court camera can take in all ten players at once. In football on TV, you can't watch the downfield patterns develop or the linebackers dropping into coverage; you just watch the ball.

Yes, at the stadium, you can take it all in. But on TV, you eventually see more.

And so on Sunday, on another one of those bright, breezy 68-degree fall afternoons, RFK Stadium again filled up and I again flopped down. Washington played Dallas, and I had a seat I wouldn't trade with Jack Kent Cooke.

After the Redskins won, then the late games came on—Eagles-Rams on CBS and Steelers-Raiders on NBC—and I sat back and kept watching.

I did get a bit restless—I actually thought of going outside at halftime—and even got a bit tired. (There's something about adulthood that seems to diminish even the purest joys.) I kept watching, though, both enduring and enjoying the games. I stayed to the end, if not as thrilled and captivated as I once was. But it was still the NFL, and there were still kids down my block sitting wide-eyed and wonder-struck at the Sunday TV spectacle.

Cable's Just Another Four-Letter Word

It's National Cable Month!!! ("Give me a C, give me an N, give me a B, give me a C, What do you got? Cable No Body Sees. C-N-B-C!!!")

I love this country.

We've got drive-thru restaurants, drive-thru banks, drive-thru liquor stores, drive-thru wedding chapels. We've got drive-in movies and drive-by shootings. We've got driving ranges, and we've got pitch 'n' putt. We've got Madonna. We've got two Michaels. We've got Super Big Gulps. We've got Call Waiting and Caller ID. We've got HelmetCam. We've got an army that hung up a pretty swift "W" with that Microwave War in the Gulf.

And we've got cable!

April is National Cable Month!!!

Him: "Honey, I've got great news."

Her: "What, dear?"

Him: "I'm taking Friday off to give us a three-day weekend and I thought . . ."

Her: "Yes?"

Him: "I thought we'd go to that Econo Lodge on Route 1 and just watch cable movies and CNN all weekend. It's National Cable Month!"

Her: "Darling, my darling, you are everything I could ever want and more. Can we get SpectraVision, too?"

Him: "Of course. I love you. You're my cable gal."

(That dialogue conjures up memories of my erstwhile marriage, which took a turn for the worse on the fourth night of our honeymoon when I had us switch to the hotel across the street because its billboard advertised FREE HBO IN ROOM. My bride at the time, who currently is my ex-wife, demanded that I make a choice. "It's either cable or it's me," she said. After scanning the program guide very briefly, I told her unequivocably, "It's you, baby doll, until eight-oh-five Friday night, TBS time." She apparently did not hear my answer, being that she already was flipping through the yellow pages in search of "Annulments.")

Ah, cable—you can't live with it, you can't live without it really getting on your nerves almost all of the time. But, hey, say what you will about cable—and that's exactly what I'm about to do—but most people who get it miss it once it's gone.

Let's go to *Webster's New World Dictionary, Third College Edition* to define this thing:

CABLE TV 1) a television system in which a high antenna and one or more dish antennas receive signals from distant and local stations, electronic satellite relays, etc. and transmit them by direct cable to the receivers of persons subscribing to the system; 2) sole livelihood for Chris Berman; 3) a pimple on the ass of civilization.

For home viewers, cable is divided into two broad categories: the cable systems that provide us with the service, and the actual cable programming.

(For those of you concerned with the quality of this essay so far, please take into consideration that as I compose this, I am also watching the Home Shopping Network in the background and have only ninety seconds left to decide whether to purchase the Amcor Ionizer Air Cleaner—retail value $99.95, priced today at $69, or three easy payments of $23—and that this type of deadline decision-making likely is adversely affecting my deadline writing skills.)

Arguably, the biggest problem with cable is dealing with your local cable system operator. Understand this about cable people: It's the cast of *Revenge of the Nerds* armed with invoices.

There is regular time and there is cable time. In regular time, things get done within a reasonable framework of your life. In cable time, things usually don't get done, and when they do, it's like when you stop at that country-road gas station and the guy comes out with the baseball cap on backward and takes somewhere in the 35-to-40-minute range to fill up your gas tank, check your oil and wipe your windshield.

You make an appointment with your dentist and you're told to be there at 10:30 A.M. sharp. You make an appointment with your cable repairman and you're told he'll be there between 12 and 6 P.M., give or take a day.

Everyone in cable is a vice president. The typical local cable system has a CEO, forty-six vice presidents and two receptionists named Shirley who answer the phone between 11:25 A.M. and 12:15 P.M. (Yes, I'm sure most of you are familiar with actually trying to call your cable system with a complaint or problem. One of three things happens—1, the phone rings forever; 2, the phone is busy forever; 3, an answering machine picks up and puts you on hold forever. Once, while I was waiting on hold, my cable system dropped the Disney Channel, added Bravo, Univision and AP Business Plus and sent me a bill upping the monthly rate by $2.25.)

As far as cable programming goes, does the term "unfulfilled potential" come to mind? Cable, indeed, is a 24-hour video convenience store, but there's nothing you really want to buy. So, just as you'll often walk out of that other 24-hour convenience store with a Slim Jim, you'll often be sitting in front of your cable box watching "Family Double Dare."

Cable, in fact, is good for only three things—sports, movies and better reception. And take away ESPN and cable suddenly looks like a Baskin-Robbins with only twenty-one flavors.

By the way, I got that Amcor air cleaner. Hey, you've got to take advantage of good deals during National Cable Month.

It's Still
a "Wide World"
on Saturdays

It was a slow and sluggish sports TV weekend, the type that makes me realize that one day in the not-so-distant future, I'll get up to fix a vertical-hold problem and, instead of stopping at the TV set, just step right out through the living room window and onto the street and never look back. I'll walk through all types of traffic. I'll walk by stores where every item every day is 50 percent off. I'll walk around week-old Slurpee cups and empty gum wrappers and still-burning cigarette butts. I'll walk until I get to Walden Pond. I'll build a cabin and I'll just sit there transcendentally for the rest of my life, unless a condo developer makes me a good offer. I will eat sunflower seeds, and I will be at peace.

Then again, there's always "Wide World of Sports."

It happened again to me Saturday afternoon, as it has happened to millions upon millions of viewers since 1961. I simply had flipped over mindlessly to ABC, and without warning, looked in on a piece of the world I never would've seen otherwise. And a weary weekend briefly was transformed into a stunning spectacle of sport.

I speak, naturally, of the Grand National Steeplechase from Aintree, England.

On a rainy day from a distant land in an event foreign to most of us, ABC reminded me how well its "Wide World" can carry viewers to sensational sights.

In just twenty minutes' time, ABC set up the event, explained its idiosyncrasies and chronicled the 144th running of the longest horse race in the world. At its best, ABC still does this type of thing better than anyone—it introduces oddities and personalities in sports with which we're largely unfamiliar, so that when things get under way, viewers feel some level of comfort with the proceedings.

Of course, it helps if Frank Gifford has the day off.

ABC made clear to the viewer how these steeplechase horses were considerably larger than typical American race horses, how the track there was much bigger than Belmont, how betting through bookmakers differed from U.S. tracks. To demonstrate the difficulty of the biggest steeplechase fences in the world, ABC analyst Lord John Oaksey—if he's a lord, he'd better be good—stood in the six-foot ditch in front of the 5-foot-2-inch fifteenth fence. It looked extraordinarily daunting.

Then this remarkable 4½-mile race began. The track is so long, three BBC announcers took turns calling the race, like a play-by-play relay team.

It was a forty-horse stampede, and at times it looked like

a posse in an old spaghetti western. There were thirty fences to negotiate and, one by one, horses and riders went down. As the race went on, the number of horses galloping along without riders rose and jockeys kept tumbling to the ground, covering up immediately to avoid being trampled.

It was a nine-minute avalanche of hoofed sound and fury, a wonder for the senses.

Of course, it helps if Frank Gifford has the day off.

When it was over, Seagram made a tremendous final run to overtake Garrison Savannah for the victory. Seagram's jockey, Nigel Hawke, was mobbed, with supporters and admirers pounding him and jostling him in his mount. (This is something I can never understand—Hawke certainly ran a good race and showed courage in his undertaking, but how about the damn horse? In heavy traffic, it just galloped four and a half miles and jumped over thirty fences with 120 pounds of grief on his back. The jockey gets all the glory, all of the money and a nice hotel bed in which to lie; the horse gets all of the oats, none of the money and a not-so-nice stable to stand in. THE HORSE DOESN'T GET DIDDLY. I mean, when was the last time you tuned in to "Lifestyles of the Rich and Famous" and saw Secretariat at his summer home in Cannes?)

The Grand National Steeplechase was the first horse race "Wide World of Sports" ever televised, back in 1962. It took me thirty years to discover it, but that's part of the appeal of "Wide World"—on any random Saturday, you might turn on the set and see the Iditarod dogsled race or Tour de France cycling or the Ironman Triathlon, and you'll be swept away into a different world for a half hour or so.

Of course, it helps if Frank Gifford has the day off.

"Wide World of Sports" acclimated a generation of Americans to watching a lot of sports television. Conceived by Roone Arledge, it was the birth of the anthology genre of sports TV—

the Column A, Column B approach to programming that gave the viewer an eclectic, erratic freedom of choice. If "Monday Night Football" created a new social dialogue and changed America's eating and sleeping habits one night a week, "Wide World" had conditioned that audience years earlier to expect sports television to be special.

Certainly, "Wide World of Sports" is a bit weathered these days. There was a time when the glow from "Wide World of Sports" could light up an entire weekend. There was a time when "Wide World of Sports" would span the globe in search of a sports world no one knew existed. There was a time when "Wide World of Sports" *was* sports television in America.

Of course, then Frank Gifford started hosting the show.

Indeed, the storied voices of "Wide World" disappeared. In a journalist-to-jock turn for the worse, broadcast luminaries Jim McKay and Howard Cosell gave way to helmet heads Gifford and Dan Dierdorf. After years of McKay's steady stewardship, having to see Frank Gifford pilot the show every week was a bit like watching Gilligan trying to steer the S.S. *Minnow.* (In 1993, Gifford finally was replaced by John Saunders, who acts as no more than a caretaker for the show.)

Actually, Gifford became only part of the problem. More than anything else, the glut of sports programming has dimmed the luster of "Wide World." All three networks air anthology series, and ESPN essentially is a twenty-four-hour anthology programmer. On many weekends, "Wide World" is just another face in the sporting crowd.

"Wide World of Sports" no longer is so much singular as it is survivor. It's not as special anymore, but it still can captivate a crowd here and there with an odd steeplechase like the Grand National. Sure, there's often too much of Lynn Swann and Jack Arute and Cheryl Miller and Bart Conner and other broadcast pretenders, but when those faces and voices exasperate and frustrate the viewer, you simply turn elsewhere.

Then again, there's always Thoreau's "Civil Disobedience."

Radio Paints
a Baseball Picture
No Big-Screen TV
Can Match

I dropped by a friend's house recently for a Mets-Braves game on TBS. We were watching—make that worshiping—this temple-like 27-inch color screen. It was a sharper, more sensational picture than any I've ever seen, with Dwight Gooden and Tom Glavine engaged in a taut pitchers' duel. But with Atlanta leading by 1–0 in the fifth inning, my friend asked if I wanted to go out for some pizza. Without a moment's thought, I said yes. And so we left, and left behind a game to which we did not return.

Late that night, as I drove home, I dialed around my car

radio in search of a baseball game. I found the Pirates-Giants game on KDKA-1020 in Pittsburgh. The signal faded in and out. But it was strong enough and compelling enough that when I reached my block, I drove past my apartment so that I could continue listening to the game.

Therein lies the difference between baseball on television and baseball on radio: One invites uninterest, the other demands attention.

On TV, baseball often is flat and listless. It doesn't jump off the screen so much as just occupy it. Announcers, often ex-players, add to the dulling, dimming effect. Yes, there are incomparable moments—like Kirk Gibson's improbable World Series homer in 1988—but much of the time, the game just lies there. Baseball's no more than background noise on a living room set; you can go about your business and then look in every once in a while to see what's happening. On TV, the game is more replay than byplay. For all its technology, TV can't pick up the nuances of the game as they occur.

"When I'm watching a TV game sitting by myself on the sofa, I have trouble staying up," said Jack Buck, who began broadcasting St. Louis Cardinals games in 1954. "Radio's different—the sounds, the announcer's voice, the crowd. There's a certain life to it, a certain vitality you don't get on television . . . For a broadcaster, it gives you a chance to emote. It's in your lap. You're not just augmenting the picture."

On a telecast, you can only see a few things; on radio, you see the whole field.

Baseball remains a radio marvel. In the video age, baseball *sounds* as good as ever. The game jumps off the dial, largely through the skills of warm, resonant voices such as Vin Scully and Jack Buck and Ernie Harwell and Jon Miller, who impart more detail than any picture in living color. It is the power of description—the ability to convey all the detailed scenery surrounding a game—that distinguishes baseball's best broadcasters. On radio, no detail is too small.

"I'm in Baltimore and when Cal Ripken comes up, everyone knows he's right-handed," said Miller, voice of the Orioles since 1983. "But I've found that in the course of saying he's right-handed, that, too, is a little picture you create in [listeners'] minds. When I say, 'Right-handed hitter, deep in the box, feet apart,' it jogs the memory for the listener, gives you a vision from which to build. I can cause you to see that dirt around home plate, the lines around the batter's box."

Scully, a protégé of the late Red Barber, worked with Barber and Connie Desmond on Brooklyn Dodgers broadcasts in the early 1950s. On road trips, one of the broadcasters usually stayed home, as Scully did during one pennant-race game. He remembers Barber's call:

"Red and Connie were working in Boston at Braves Field. I was at home listening. It was a pivotal game, an important game. Well, Red saw this storm brewing off a ways. He began weaving in the story about the game and the storm. The Dodgers were leading by a run and it wasn't an official game yet. He kept driving home the point that this game might not be completed in time.

"By the fifth inning, he had you waiting on the storm. As the storm approached the stadium, he proceeded to go into great detail about it, all the while keeping up with the details of the game. It reached the point where I felt that I could almost smell the rain in the air.

"Finally, there were two out in the [Braves'] fifth, the Dodgers up by a run. Red had the raindrops hitting the outfield wall. Now he had the rain stretching across the outfield, all the while stressing that as soon as this storm hit, the game would be over.

"Well, I forget who was up, and usually it would be expected that the batter would stall around the plate, trying to buy some time, but inexplicably, he swung at the pitch, a grounder to the shortstop. Red had the raindrops on the bill of Pee Wee Reese's cap as he fielded the ball and he had the rain crossing the infield as [first baseman Gil] Hodges caught the ball. And with that third out, he says, 'And here comes the storm, and there will be no more baseball today.'

"And he was right."

As Scully's story demonstrates, radio draws in the listener. You can hear a foul ball crash up against the broadcast booth behind the plate; on TV, it just flashes out of sight. If you're watching a game on TV with somebody else, your conversation often overshadows the announcers'. But when listening to the radio, you tend to talk only during commercial breaks.

What's more, radio is a companion. TV's there much of the time—actually, maybe too much—but radio's there every night. It's an April-to-September constant: You finish dinner, you turn on the game; you're driving home from the movies, you turn on the game; you have absolutely nothing to do, you turn on the game. What kid who grew up in the East following baseball doesn't remember lying in bed late at night, trying to stay awake to listen to the home team playing a West Coast game?

Perhaps most important, radio goes where TV can't—the highway:

You're on the road, in a rusting '82 Ford Maverick, battling the heat and the boredom and the truckers on the turnpike, just beyond neoscenic Breezewood, Pennsylvania. It's still a long way to Cincinnati, when suddenly, the sounds of your car radio cut through the thick night air and bring a smile to your ears. It's Harry Kalas or Marty Brennaman or Milo Hamilton. The static may be crackling, but it's the sweetest sound on the road. If you're lucky, the game of the moment could take you all the way into Ohio.

It's the magic of the medium—after dark, when certain stations go off the air and other stations are allowed to increase the power of their signals, distant cities become as close as your dashboard. And so the much-maligned AM dial remains a flight of fancy on a trip of tiresome toll roads. Sure, when driving on a long, lonely journey it's nice to hear Bruce Springsteen telling us that we're all born to run, but it's better to hear Jack Buck tell us that Vince Coleman's going to run.

"To me," Miller said, "Jack Buck's voice on the radio is baseball. You hear it and you know there's a ball game on."

Which is not to say that you should turn off the TV the next time a baseball game comes on. It is to say that given the choice between watching on a projection screen or a transistor radio, you'll see the game a lot better with your eyes closed.

If It Sounds
Like Chicken-Fried Steak,
It Just Might Be
Keith Jackson

When ABC's Keith Jackson first started broadcasting college football, folks wore raccoon coats to games, carried pennants and screamed "Hubba, hubba!" Stadium grandstands filled with rich and fat men drinking in their past and drinking to their future.

But nowadays, with the advent of cable television, these alumni can do the same thing by simply staying at home, and, better yet, they save on cleaning costs for the raccoon coats.

Of course, Jackson still goes on-campus to go on-air.

Exactly what he's saying, I've never been quite sure—until this year, that is, when I inexplicably rushed back to those autumn Saturday afternoons on TV like some Chris Schenkel infatuate.

I always have felt about college football as I do about the governments of Brazil: They should live and be well.

I had given up on college football some time ago. For one thing, I'm not in college anymore. For another, most games mean nothing. There's an old criticism about the NBA that you only have to tune in for the last two minutes of any game; well, with college football, you only have to wake up two minutes before the New Year's Day bowl fest commences. And even if you miss that, you only need to check "SportsCenter" the next day and you're all caught up.

So I skipped the 1980s—meaning I missed Miami—and when I made it back in the nineties, Keith Jackson was right where I left him, sounding so much the hog caller at a county fair.

My main problem with Jackson always had been this: I could make out most of the words, but I couldn't understand the meaning. It's as if he had created his own world with his own language, and you couldn't visit that world unless you could conjugate the various Keithisms.

He sighs. He emotes. He growls. He elongates certain syllables. He has a cadence all his own. He is from a school of broadcasting that may never have existed. He bumps and grinds through a telecast, like a reliable old car with a rough engine that never seems as if it's going to get to where it's going, yet always pulls up right in the nick of time.

Most of all, he speaks the rhythms of college football—or at least the myth of college football—with his trace-of-Dixie accent and homespun, greens-and-grits manner. He just seems like the type of guy who spends the first few hours of the day tailgating. Autumn leaves don't fall until Jackson calls an Auburn touchdown. And even though he works plenty of Pac-10 games (and lives just outside Los Angeles), he always sounds like he's in Tallahassee or Tuscaloosa.

Jackson certainly didn't sound right during his one year (1970) on "Monday Night Football"—he's country time, not prime time—and he was a bust on baseball. He's not a flawless technician of play-by-play. But on college football, surrounded by painted faces and fusty pageantry, Jackson—ABC's No. 1 announcer on the sport since 1976—just might be the past imperfect voice for an imperfect setting.

At the Rose Bowl one year, after a Washington receiver dropped a pass while being viciously hit by a Michigan defender, Jackson offered: "That's probably like trying to brush your teeth in a twelve-foot boat with a nine-foot wave."

Another time, during a Washington-Stanford game, after the Husky quarterback scrambled before finding a receiver for a score, Jackson intoned: "The Stanford defense did everything in the world but hang him on a sycamore tree and he still got the touchdown."

During a Michigan-Indiana game, the Hoosiers muffed a ball that bounded into the end zone. Indiana picked up the ball as Michigan players rushed toward it, prompting Jackson to say: "That's a piece of lemon meringue pie waiting for a white shirt."

Unfortunately, I never have a Keith-to-English dictionary readily available.

But eventually, even if you don't know a word of a particular language, you pick it up if it's the only tongue spoken. And on Saturday afternoons from September to December, you either become fluent in Keith Jackson or you simply don't know the score.

Actually, I'm starting to like the guy, which is starting to worry me.

If nothing else, you do get the sense he's seen more than

one game in his time. He lends some perspective. So that recently, after one unbeaten team defeated another in an early-season game and folks immediately began shouting about who the best team in the land was, Jackson simply surmised:

"All this hoop-de-doo and yakety-yak over who's number one right now doesn't mean a dad-gum thing."

From what I can gather, that makes a whole lot of horse sense.

With Cruise Control, Maybe I Can Speed Past Auto Racing Next Time

T wice a year, as part of my contractual agreement to be the conscience of America's sports-viewing commu-nity, I am strapped into my recliner and forced to watch auto racing, the greased-up game of the great unwashed. I speak, of course, of the Daytona 500 and the Indianapolis 500, in which those twin American passions of speed and violence collide just a few paces away from tens of thousands of bare-chested, beer-bellied good ol' boys waving the flag and smoking some Marlboros.

It would help if I had an air bag.

Now, I suspect that some of you out there—particularly

the ones who usually honk because I'm doing only thirty-five mph in the left lane of the interstate—are wary of my auto racing credentials. In the spirit of self-disclosure, I guess it's important to detail my general auto racing ignorance/bias:

(1) Like many others, I usually prefer to watch just one car race a year—the chase scene in *Bullitt.*

(2) It seems to me that every pit crew has a guy named Bubba.

(3) Who keeps track of the laps?

(4) From what I can tell, the green flag means full speed, the yellow flag means caution and the black flag means there's a dead bug on the windshield.

Who can watch auto racing on TV, anyway? They go around and around and around the track, and it's awful hard to pick up their license plates at that speed. You have no idea what's going on. It's like watching an air raid at an anthill. Plus, *you* try watching the Indy 500 after spending two months watching America's Cup; it feels like a football game in fast-forward.

This remains one sport in which you cannot ignore the announcers. With the sound down, you have absolutely no idea what's going on. But frankly, with the sound up, I'm not exactly sure what they're saying. Autospeak makes Latin look livable.

They talk about brake rotors and rear-wheel bearings and loose chassis and fuel cells and overhead cam engines and tread width and oiler cooler blockage and defusers and rear-end gear malfunctions and turbocharged V6s. And the announcers keep talking about this "drafting" business, how autos would "draft" off each other. (Is that why so many cars with New Jersey plates are tailgating me on every highway in America?)

Curiously—well, curiously to me, that is—nobody ever brings up Fahrvergnugen. (That's "far-fair-gnu-ghen," or as Indy fans pronounce it, "slow German car." Believe you me: All these fancy cars that rush into pit row with engine problems, they'd be OK if they had Fahrvergnugen. It's like the old tortoise-and-hare story. I guarantee you—put a VW Bug out there, have it putter along the left lane of the speedway, and while all those hotshots scrape the wall at unthinkable speeds, that Beetle will make it to Victory Lane. I've got friends with Bugs nearing the 200,000-mile mark; what's another 500 on a clear day?)

Let's get it straight right here and now: Life is too short to be able to say "Chris Economaki" at any point of any day.

And how about that Sam Posey? Sam was opining at the Indy 500 that the reason there are so few injuries with so many crashes indicates improved safety features on Indy cars, and he said he hoped the technology would be passed on to passenger cars in the next ten years. Yo, Sam, speaking for all passenger-car drivers, we'd just be happy to find auto mechanics who get us our car back by Friday. I mean, I don't get it: When I have to take my car into the shop, the mechanic will call me with an estimate a day or two later—always some incredibly inflated figure—and then, if I'm lucky, I see the car again by month's end. At Daytona and Indy, these guys roll into a pit stop, get their tires changed, oil checked, gas tank filled and windshield-wiper fluid replaced—and WHOOOOOOOOOSH—they're back out on the road in under twenty seconds. And there's no charge!

I will say this: Those Daytona and Indy mechanics are just like mine in that no matter what they do to the car, you always have to bring it back in with the same problem. Heck, one year at Indy, cars were dropping out before the race even *began*. You think these babies even passed inspection? Meanwhile, competitors were coming in with so many automotive ailments, you would've thought they were all driving Chryslers. And others out on the track were spinning out one after another, undoubtedly causing car insurance premiums for you and me to skyrocket.

The announcers—ABC's Posey, Paul Page and Bobby Unser on the Indy and CBS's Economaki, Mike Joy and Ken Squier on the Daytona—always talk about the courage of the competitors and the spectacular improvements in the cars they drive. But the question remains: Are these fellows great athletes, or are they just passengers aboard technologically great machines?

I don't want to belittle the skills of these three dozen or so individuals racing 200 mph around a dangerous oval, but I've seen more daredevil driving feats during morning rush hour when various folks go bumper-to-bumper at high speeds while either combing their hair, putting on makeup or reading the paper.

The Daytona and Indy both have their drawbacks as viewing extravaganzas.

Every year we get that Daytona-500-is-a-piece-of-Americana bit. It's our patriotic duty, according to NASCAR and CBS, to watch this slice-of-American-life race.

The Daytona doctrine tells us that this is somehow the people's race. Indy-style cars, after all, are made out of aluminum foil and are driven by rich kids. Stock cars look just like the ones you and I can go out and buy and are driven by regular good guys. This is the great American race that appeals to a dwindling breed of American—that self-reliant, rural, ram-tough Marlboro man who is a descendant of those who once tamed the old frontier. Open land, running free. These racers, from the heartland of America, speak to the restlessness and independence of spirit of this great nation (this you never hear about bowlers).

So, while you're sitting at home with your cellular phone, Brie cheese, Evian water and BMW, you just watch this high-speed spectacle where everybody still has a Chevy, and somehow you've bought into America.

Forget, of course, that these people are more in bed with corporate sponsors than anyone else in sport. Every inch of their bodies is for sale. They're good for more plugs than Champion. They'll literally change hats during postrace interviews to take care of more business. Tobacco and beer companies are the lifeblood of auto racing (yes, drinking and driving can mix, so long as you know when to say "When do you want the money?")

Is there any greater sight in sport than watching the Levi Strauss car edge the Snickers car at the finish line?

On the positive end of CBS's Daytona 500, there is the steady lap-by-lap broadcasting of Squier and, of course, those incredible in-car cameras—the racecam, facecam, bumpercam and pitcam. (Future coverage will include a "nolo cam" for those drivers who choose not to contest the race any longer and a "cam cam," a French idea being adapted for American use.)

I also have a soft spot in my heart for Economaki, but then again, I don't even use my heart that much anymore.

As for ABC's Indy 500 coverage, the biggest problem is that it is in "stereophonic sound," which means that the combination of the race cars, Sam Posey and the crowd noise make the telecast sound somewhat like an Aerosmith concert.

It also would help if ABC actually would show us the end of the race, a small problem that occurred in 1992 when the network missed the closest finish in Indy 500 history because of a bad camera cut. I didn't mind too much; after all, I got to see the finish—Al Unser edging Scott Goodyear by .043 of a second—on a Valvoline commercial a month later.

There are two other ABC announcing problems: Page isn't as steady a hand as Squier, and Jack Arute isn't as steady an interviewer as, say, Ahmad Rashad.

Arute does yeoman's service as ABC's pit boss all day, but then he is asked to interview the winner afterward. In '92 as he talked with Al Unser, Jr., it occurred to me that Arute would be better working a 900 love line than conducting an interview. And then there was 1990, when Arie Luyendyk won, and here were Arute's five "questions":

- "Arie Luyendyk, welcome to the Indy 500 Victory Lane."

- "The race came to you today."

- "You're not perspiring. . . . You don't even seem like this was much of a five-hundred-mile contest for you."

- "Your name goes into the record book" (for highest average speed).

- "Was it an emotional moment when you took the checkered flag?"

Reminder: Those were all questions.

Here's a TV question of my own: Whatever happened to "Speed Racer"?

It's a Bird,
It's a Blimp,
No—It's
George Foreman!

George Foreman is gaining.

He's gaining acceptance as a legitimate heavy-weight fighter.

He's gaining favor as a popular HBO boxing analyst.

He's gaining recognition as an engaging talk-show guest.

He's gaining quite a sizable income.

He's gaining weight, of course.

All the while—and I know this doesn't matter all that much in the big picture—he's gaining my approval. I would also contend that if Big George is gaining all of the above, the rest of us are losing something, whether we know it or not.

From the beginning of his improbable comeback tour—a.k.a. the Tour de Flesh—Foreman appeared to me to be just a fat and immovable preacher-turned-creature feature, a marketing and media creation designed to eventually fool the public at $39.95 a pop. But somehow, he has gone from bloated burlesque act to HBO headliner, from Burger King prop to pay-per-view champ.

And, unbelievably, I'm one of those who's paying to view him.

This much I still believe:

(1) George Foreman cannot fight.

(2) Anytime he does fight, I cannot fight the feeling that I want to watch him.

Sure, Foreman can punch, provided the target is stationary, dead or Gerry Cooney. But he has no lateral mobility. He has no forward or backward mobility. He has no mobility whatsoever. If someone yelled "Fire!" in a crowded theater, Foreman would just watch the rest of the film. He is old and he is obese. His body is swollen like a beach ball. The reason he eats so much is because it cuts down on the amount of time between meals, and he really has nothing to do between meals other than to snack.

Here's the tale of the tape that all of the newspapers run these days on Foreman: age, fortysomething; height, 6-foot-4; weight, 250–275; reach, 79 inches; chest (normal), 47 inches; chest (expanded), 49 inches; biceps, 17 inches; waist, 38 ½ inches; thigh, 28 ½ inches; calf, 20 inches; neck, 18 inches.

Here's the tale of the tape on Foreman you *won't* see: cholesterol count, 248; riboflavin content, 34; polyunsaturated fat, 5,500–6,000; estimated walking time between dining room and kitchen, 54 seconds; proximity to McDonald's, 1.2 miles;

driving time between home and McDonald's (normal), 4 minutes, 25 seconds; driving time between home and McDonald's (rush hour), 4 minutes, 57 seconds; average number of times returns to breakfast buffet at Denny's, 6; chicken thighs, calves and necks consumed during final week of training, 66.

Let's have a quick George Foreman quiz!

Group One: James Mitchell, Christian Herter, Charles Wilson, Thomas Gates and Marion Folsom. Group Two: Timothy Anderson, Richard Sekorski, Charles Hostetter, Mark Young and Robert Hitzelburg. Which group contains names of boxers George Foreman beat on his comeback tour, and which group contains names of cabinet members during Dwight Eisenhower's presidential tour? (Quiz answer to follow a bit later.)

If you tapped Foreman's comeback opponents on the shoulder and asked them for the time of day, most of them would fall down.

Foreman's plump promenade toward heavyweight prominence worked like this: First, he gets twenty-odd straight wins against handpicked pugs. Out of sight of most people, his reputation grows, and with pay-per-view and premium cable always in search of big names, Foreman becomes marketable. Along the way he's matched against another marquee mistake, Gerry Cooney. National publications and newspapers, always fast to create new heroes, hype the fight. This heightens interest and lends credibility to the fight, which in turn draws a bigger TV audience. Promoters sell more tickets, TV folks get more viewers, papers sell more copies, all of which translates to more money being made. Foreman batters Cooney—who is knocked down regularly by his own punching bag—and the legend grows.

(Quiz answer: Group One names are from Eisenhower's cabinet; none of them ever fought professionally.)

When Foreman finally stepped into the ring against then-champion Evander Holyfield, I figured Foreman's boxing future was just a few minutes from being over.

I was wrong.

Foreman lasted twelve rounds with Holyfield; people talked about the fight for weeks before and after. In a crowded and cheapened entertainment environment, it was truly a "moment." And even if you have to manufacture these moments, the public—which wants the larger-than-life matchup, the occasional release from the mundane—doesn't seem to mind.

Regrettably, I believe I have become part of that public. (I think it's due to too much time eating at 7-Elevens, browsing at Crown Books and glancing at *USA Today*.)

The public—and I was out there, on street corners, with the rest of the madding crowd—talked about what a terrific fight it was. Hey, Foreman-Holyfield was no Ali-Frazier. But people don't mind being fooled, particularly if everyone else is fooled along with them; then, nobody can tell the difference between a classic and a clinker. There's a lot of stuff out there that's mediocre that passes for magnificent these days, and it has all to do with money and the making of gobs and gobs and gobs of it.

And so it goes: Foreman suddenly is an attraction. How can this happen? Well, in the brilliant film *Broadcast News,* I recall the Albert Brooks character telling the Holly Hunter character that the danger of the William Hurt character—a rising network news star with absolutely no journalistic background or moral center—was that slowly and sometimes imperceptibly guys like him would lower our standards, until you look down and you don't know how you got from there to here.

Gosh, I do like George. I like watching him fight and I like watching him talk and I even like watching him eat. He's become enormously popular entertainment. In fact, there he is now, trying to star in a sitcom with Tony Danza—Tony

Danza!—as executive producer. You know, somehow a George Foreman-Tony Danza collaboration on TV doesn't conjure up memories of Carroll O'Connor-Norman Lear or Mary Tyler Moore-James L. Brooks. But, sure enough, if Foreman makes it into prime time, a lot of critics and a lot of the public will like it a lot, and there'll even be a laugh track piped in to make sure everyone knows it's a damn funny show. And if everyone's laughing, it must be funny.

Sports News
These Days
Is Just the
Tale of the Tape

You're in Houston or Baltimore or Seattle or Louisville or Cleveland or Memphis, watching the late local news. And at twenty minutes past the hour, Michael Jordan—who may not have played a good game, whose team may not have won, who may not have even been a major factor in deciding the outcome—is going to streak down the court for one of his countless acrobatic slam dunks.

Welcome to the valley of the videotape, a seemingly endless stretch of sports highlights that takes newscast viewers from the weather to the wee hours. And no matter where you may be across America, on TV sets small and large, it always looks and sounds the same. It's the Muzak of the nineties.

Where have all the local sportscasts gone? Gone are the days of just reading scores, gone are the days of pursuing stories and interviews, gone are the days of talking endlessly into the camera. It's the Shake-Rattle-'n'-Roll Era of local TV sports, where a blooper is worth a thousand words and no news is good news.

The only thing that counts is having good tape. If they have it, they show it; if they don't, they won't be in town for long.

Hello, highlights. Bye-bye, news.

You'd better get used to those rousing rodeo clips.

For this, the credit or blame, in part, can go to ESPN.

With its thrice-nightly "SportsCenter," ESPN has broadened interest in the national sporting scene over the past decade. ESPN has made more viewers—and news stations—nationally conscious and has thus increased the appetite for highlights from all over. In a way, ESPN sets the agenda for tape. TV is a very insecure, derivative medium, so whatever is working for ESPN, local sports operations figure, can work for them, too.

ESPN also does some features and interviews, because it has a half hour. Local sportscasts, meanwhile, generally get the same amount of time today as yesterday. But whereas ten years ago local sportscasters may have chased local stories and may have done interviews and might have even given occasional commentaries, in the nineties they devote a disproportionate amount of time to highlights.

So while many sportscasters once tried to establish a clear-cut identity, their primary identity now is tape.

It's safe to go to the tape. The formula local sportscast these days consists of the following ingredients: (1) Make chitchat with the anchor; (2) Celebrate the home team; (3) Don't antagonize anyone; (4) Go to the videotape; (5) Rinse and repeat.

These fellows never take a position, they never threaten their paycheck, they don't ask any questions that don't have easy answers. The serious stuff gets short shrift. Sportscasters, once journalists of sorts, are closer in spirit these days to Tom Jones than to Tom Brokaw. They each develop their own lounge act—revolving around the videotape—and the best of them bring the crowd back again and again.

ESPN's presence creates another problem: With many serious sports fans turning to the all-sports cable network for their news, that leaves local sportscasters scrambling for an audience. If these sportscasters can't hold on to the sports fans, they then go after the non-sports viewers tuning in to local news, and they do that with an array of odd clips and bizarre highlights to create a video freak show of sorts.

TV types used to get many of their stories from newspapers. The local daily might report one morning that a star player is disgruntled; the local stations then would put him on camera on the news that evening. But those sportscasters don't even have to read anymore, other than following the script on the TelePrompTer.

Actually, it makes sense.

First of all, it's easier for a sportscaster to collect what comes off the satellite dish or to subscribe to a highlights service than it is to develop stories or chase news leads.

Secondly, the rush for replays is justified by the unmistakable fact that TV, after all, is a visual medium.

Finally, as disturbing as it may be, those highlights are exactly what most viewers want, anyway.

At its core, sports is still just who won, who lost and who made the big play; it's easiest to tell the tale through tape. And most sportscasters are going to shy away from the complex story that doesn't wear well on TV. The sports fan, given the choice of watching some issue-oriented commentary or seeing videotape of any game, is going to take the highlight reel almost every time.

The disc jockey on Top 40 radio finds an audience by playing the same songs over and over; the video jock on sportscasts plays on that same viewer's desire to be fed the familiar. When Jordan dribbles downcourt and dunks for the umpteenth time on the eleven o'clock news, viewers' expectations are fulfilled. Viewers find it comforting to see the same highlight tonight that they saw last night.

What happens, though, is that viewers lose context. Every time Bo Jackson breaks his bat over his knee, that's the highlight that makes the news; whatever else might be happening to Jackson's team gets glossed over. In any given week of running catches and long home runs, it becomes difficult to separate the significant from the superfluous. On TV, all jump shots were created equal, so who can tell one from another?

But then again, if it's all the same to you, what's good enough one night is good enough the next.

Those Misty Watercolor Memories of the Way We Were (Before Sports TV)

The following story is true, with minor embellishment in key spots. Names are not changed because, hey, nobody's innocent anymore.

We stood on the pier and looked out beyond the future. She saw a new life; I saw the Super Bowl on pay-per-view. Tears welled up in her eyes, and soon it was as if two bathtubs were overflowing with hot water. I was distracted, partly by the 40-mph winds and partly by the Tigers-Red Sox game I was listening to on my Sony Walkman.

A gust came up and blew my sunglasses into the water.

Her sobbing turned to crying, and her cries turned to wails, and her wailing became irritating. I couldn't hear Ernie Harwell. I had had enough. I started to walk away.

"Go on," she shouted. "Go back to your Brent and your Marv and your Giff."

I turned around angrily.

"Listen, babe," I said icily. "In the first place, I don't listen to Giff. And in the second place, you've got no business calling him Giff. You've got no right. Only Cosell should call him Giff."

"Cosell called him The Giffer," she responded.

"A lot you know," I said with a sniff. "You were watching 'Mayberry R.F.D.' every Monday night."

She glared at me contemptuously. She resented the years of "The NFL Today," the Game of the Week, Chris Schenkel and Keith Jackson, "Wide World of Sports," and, most of all, the PBA Tour. And just as she had finally adjusted, cable came. She hated cable like an inchworm hates a hill. "Cable kills," she once had proclaimed as she maniacally tried to dig it up from our backyard.

Now, she edged to the end of the pier.

"You can shove your playoffs, your pregame shows and your telestrators. You want TV dinners? Now you've got them," she cried out. "I hope you have a vertical-hold problem for the rest of your life."

And she threw herself into the water.

Panic-stricken, I raced to the end of the pier. I saw her struggling for survival.

"To your left, to your left," I shouted to her frantically, "can you see my sunglasses to your left?"

Luckily, an off-duty lifeguard came along and saved her. But he could not save a relationship gutted by the glut of sports television.

We had seen it happen to other couples. But we thought it could never happen to us. We were different. After all, not only did we have a Toshiba 26-inch stereo TV with MTS/dbx decoder, 27-key direct access remote control, 122-channel capability and 400 lines of horizontal resolution—what a picture!!—but we also had each other. We were in love, and not even the specter of high-definition TV could come between us.

Yet I had ignored the warning signs from the start. Some would say I saw just what I wanted to see. Some would say I created the danger zones. But was it my fault that our wedding fell on Derby Day? Guests still marvel at the remarkable timing of how they could hear ABC's Dave Johnson screaming, "And down the stretch they come!!" just as the bridal party made its way toward the altar. And even if I were watching the race—a fact never proven conclusively—it was not I who had turned on the TV set.

Somehow, the love left us a few thousand TV time-outs later on a bright winter afternoon, seemingly a day to rejoice as no other. We had gone to Fabrizio's Bistro for a rare double celebration: She had gotten an important job promotion and I had found out that ESPN would be televising 175 baseball games a year. We took that romantic corner booth near the bar, where I had a good view of a Golden State-Atlanta NBA game on the 40-inch projection TV screen. I had my woman and I had my Warriors, and at that moment I thought I just might be the luckiest man on Earth.

Not so.

As she sipped her wine—a semidry yet crisp Sicilian red— she spat out several years of video venom against me. She recalled the shortwave radio I brought along on our honeymoon. She produced a pirated Nielsen diary indicating 245 consecutive days of sports viewing. She leveled me, from sign-on to sign-off. It was a bad scene, best indicated by the fact that two lawyers quietly slipped their business cards onto our table.

The maître d' approached.

"Is everything satisfactory, sir?"

I struggled to answer civilly.

"The veal's a little tough, my wife's a little upset and our view of the screen is blocked as you stand there. Otherwise, everything's super. Check, please."

We left with just over four minutes remaining in the game and the Warriors trailing by three.

Not many weeks later, we found ourselves taking that long walk on that short pier. And as she emerged from the water, I realized it was over. She still loved me—she had the sunglasses in hand—but she couldn't live with me anymore, that much was clear. I mouthed a good-bye to her shivering figure and turned away.

It would be a tough, lonely night ahead. Thank goodness I had taped "SportsWorld."

I Like a 0–0 Soccer Match as Much as the Next Guy Not Watching It

Remember when soccer was going to be the sport of the 1970s? Then it was going to be the sport of the '80s. Now, with the World Cup coming to the United States in 1994, it is going to be the sport of the '90s. Perhaps its boom is still a decade away—then it can be the sport of the '00s, which would be appropriate since nobody ever scores.

Rule No. 1 of American TV sports: You've got to have TV time-outs.

Rule No. 2 of American TV sports: You've got to score, score, score.

This is America. This is an action country. We watch *The*

Terminator, therefore we are. Every eighteen months or so, we attack some island nation that has no militia. This is an action country. Do you remember the ABC show "The Mackenzies of Paradise Cove"? Of course you don't; it lasted through about two commercial breaks. It was about some crusty old fishing-boat operator in Hawaii who became sort of an unofficial father to a pack of orphans whose parents were lost at sea. Too much sentiment, not enough scoring. Jack Lord wouldn't even watch it, and it was filmed in his backyard. This is an action country.

Let's go to the TV scoreboard for the last two World Cups:

In 1986, NBC's World Cup telecasts averaged a 2.2 rating, and its live telecast of the Argentina-West Germany final drew a 4.1 (numbers represent the percentage of TV homes tuning in). ESPN's fifteen games averaged a microscopic 0.5 rating (percentage of cable homes tuning in). Granted, nearly every match was a 2 P.M. weekday telecast, but daily exercise shows like "Bodies in Motion" regularly do 0.6s and 0.7s on ESPN. (Repeat: That's *taped* muscle toning outdrawing *live World Cup soccer,* the most popular sporting event on the whole planet.)

In 1990, TNT did twenty-four World Cup games live, averaging a 1.2 cable rating, with its telecast of the Argentina-West Germany final drawing a 2.2. Boy, you can see how the sport is riding a wave of interest in this country; hell, the Home Shopping Network does better numbers anytime it puts zirconium cuff links on special for forty-five minutes.

Besides being a nonstop sport, soccer is not conducive to commercial television in several other ways.

Good TV sports are played in a confined space. (Pocket billiards, for instance, is a far superior TV sport to soccer.) Even in football—contested on a field similar in size to soccer's—the action generally is concentrated in a limited area on any given play. Soccer looks more like an Easter egg hunt.

There are no identifiable stars for the U.S. audience. (Can

you name one player on the United Arab Emirates team? For that matter, can you name one player on the U.S. national team? Most people still think Kyle Rote, Jr., is playing.)

In the MTV era, everything is short and fast, with quick cuts. Soccer is the antithesis of that. The key eighteen-to-thirty-four demographic group has the attention span of a pear. With wireless remotes, for soccer it's twenty-seconds-and-out.

Soccer's solution is simple, but the stodgy traditionalists won't even consider it: Everyone should be allowed to use his hands *except* the goalie. Then we'd see some run-and-shoot offense. It's simply unnatural to play a game with a ball and not be able to use one's hands. (For those of you in the suburbs, I invite you to go outside right now with a friend or family member and toss a ball toward that person. He won't try to hit the ball with his head or feet or stop it with his chest; he will try to catch it. For those of you in the city, it's not worth the risk to go out onto the streets for this experiment; just take my word for it.)

Okay, perhaps the hands thing is an unrealistic adjustment. I mean, you wouldn't go up to big-rig truck drivers and tell them they have to start signaling when changing lanes. I understand that soccer buffs want to preserve the integrity of their game. Here, then, is a reasonable five-point plan to make soccer a TV bonanza:

- Institute TV time-outs.

- Install a 24-second shot clock.

- Establish a three-point goal from 19 feet 9 inches. (This will change that whole business about a 2–0 lead being insurmountable in soccer.)

- Eliminate the live goalie. Instead, have a team member operate a life-size flatboard cutout figure in goal—like in slot hockey or Foosball—that could be maneuvered back and forth with the use of a joystick.

- Abolish all ties. Go to a sudden-death overtime format in which the team that gives up the losing goal then must have its game captain executed at midfield.

Are you listening, FIFA? In academia, it's publish or perish. In TV sports, it's score or bore. And what's the deal with these Brazilian players who just go by one name? Is Madonna the team owner, or what?

Extra, Extra:
Sportswriters Swarming
into Living Rooms!

"Looking over this panel, isn't everyone on television?"
—Bill Conlin of the *Philadelphia Daily News,* on ESPN's
"The Sports Reporters"

Once, sportswriters were merely on every street corner and outside every doorstep, available seven days a week in your local newspaper. But these days, they come into every living room and onto every sports viewer's lap, available twenty-four hours a day on television. Sportswriters have discovered television and television has discovered sportswriters, and suddenly the ink-stained wretches are a growth industry.

Boy, it's not a particularly good-looking group, now is it?

Sportswriters are upon us. They are the modern-day locust, the main difference being that sportswriters descend upon the public every seventeen minutes rather than every seventeen years.* Under certain environmental conditions, young sportswriters develop into a short-winged migratory form, gather in huge swarms, and at maturity (and sometimes before) take to the airwaves. The swarms include lowly beat reporters and princely star columnists. When they finally settle, the resulting agricultural and social devastation is enormous.

Once upon a time, sportswriters hated television. They resented its omnipresence. They resented its influence on events. They resented how cameras and microphones pushed them toward the rear of press conferences. They resented how the medium diminished their roles as conveyors of information. And, most of all, sportswriters resented TV's on-air stars, who made much more money for much less work. The TV play-by-play announcer's job ended moments after the final gun, a time when the sportswriter had to rush to the locker room, gather quotes and head back to the pressroom to write a story deep into the night.

Plus, these sports announcers had blow-dried hair, blow-dried wives and blow-dried personalities.

But now, the dirty little secret of sportswriters is out: They all wanted to be sportscasters.

The networks came calling. They found that sportswriters held an invaluable commodity—information—in an increasingly competitive environment. Who had better NFL sources than Will McDonough? Who knew more baseball people than Peter Gammons? Who was better connected in the NBA than

---

*A strong case can be made that, actually, sportswriters on TV more closely resemble the cicada than the locust. The cicada is described as a "large, noise-producing insect with a stout body, a wide blunt head, protruding eyes and two pairs of membranous wings." The male cicada "makes a loud, shrill sound," not unlike the noise often heard on sportswriter-panel talk shows. Winged adults in the cicada family, though, only live for about one week; most sportswriters usually take that long just to fill out expense reports.)

Peter Vecsey? More and more, sportswriters were called upon as expert commentators in the fields they covered.

And cable came calling. They found that sportswriters held another invaluable commodity—the ability to talk forever—in an industry constantly in search of programming. Sportswriter-panel shows were born, among them ESPN's "The Sports Reporters," SportsChannel America's "The Sports Writers on TV" and BET's "Budweiser Sports Report." Meanwhile, regional cable networks found they needed sportswriters to take phone calls from viewers over the air; this used to be called radio.

So fame-starved sportswriters these days are racing for the studio with the speed and alacrity once reserved only for press buffets. (Free cold cuts are nice, but—to use the cable terminology currently in vogue—a dual revenue stream is a lot nicer.)

For sportswriters in search of TV jobs, there's only one place to start: the *Boston Globe*. McDonough, Gammons, Bud Collins, Jackie MacMullan, Bob Ryan and Lesley Visser are all current or former *Globe* sportswriters who have splashed onto the screen nationally. At any given time at the *Globe*, half the staff is on deadline and the other half is in makeup. They don't have a newsroom, they have a greenroom. In a bygone era, most sportswriters had editors; *Globe* scribes have agents.

All across New England, responsible parents are calling in their children from various athletic playgrounds and putting them behind typewriters so that they can one day make it big on television.

Now, there's nothing really wrong with sportswriters grabbing a bit of gold for themselves like everyone else. But it robs America of one of the last romantic, underdog images of newspaper journalism—the common-man, working-stiff sportswriter, just chasing stories in the shadows of stadiums everywhere.

Slap Maxwell might have been on prime time, but he never would've done TV.

Let's Celebrate Bowling.
Yes, Bowling.

The French call it joie de vivre, a joyous celebration of life's unexpected moments.

I call it bowling on TV.

Bowling just strikes me right.

Every winter Saturday—and I know naysayers and cynics out there will tell you this is more a commentary on my life than on the merits of watching Amleto Monacelli—the ninety TV minutes I spend with the professional bowlers on ABC are the best ninety minutes of my week.

I know I am not alone in this regard. (Ask A. C. Nielsen.) So I want the rest of you to come out of your homes, shake your bowling ball bags in the air and shout out, "I'm happy as hell and I'm not going to take these 'doesn't-every-shot-on-a-bowling-telecast-look-identical?' jokes anymore."

We shouldn't be embarrassed. I mean, you'd think we all were watching fly-fishing or something. It's bowling, and let me tell you: No two snowflakes are alike and no two gutter balls are alike. It's wonderful to watch *and* an incredible number of people are watching it.

The Professional Bowlers Tour, which debuted on ABC January 6, 1962, is the cultural phenomenon of sports television. After all, besides the Flintstones and the Honeymooners, who ever bowls on TV? (You never saw Hope turn to Michael on "thirtysomething" and say, "God, how I love you. Let's go roll a few frames.") But somewhere beyond the gourmet-market lines, somewhere beyond the squash clubs, somewhere beyond "Wall Street Week," some people are bowled over by the PBT.

Its popularity has waned a bit in recent years, yet the bowlers tour still is a programming nightmare for the other networks. Bowling usually wins its time period. Bowling out-draws golf. Bowling outdraws basketball. Bowling outdraws tennis. Bowling destroys anything in its path. Hell, bowling just might kick Roseanne's butt, given the opportunity.

How can this be? Is there some deep-seated sociopolitical, synecological explanation for this plebeian manifestation?

Hey, I'm no sociologist, I'm just another 150 bowler. (Yeah, yeah, yeah, I *do* bowl. What of it? What did you think I was doing when I wasn't watching sports on TV, translating Sartre's *Being and Nothingness?* I have two different types of bowling shirts—polyester pullover and polyester button-down. I don't have my own ball and I don't have my own shoes; I've always endorsed the pay-per-shoe rental concept. I use a 14-pound ball, except when I'm drinking heavily, in which case I then switch to duckpins. I'm not up-to-date on the latest American Bowling Congress rules concerning lane-oil application, but I do hate when the oil is uneven; it's not good when you're frying eggs and it's not good when you're throwing big hooks. I picked up the 7–10 split once, but it was disallowed because the ball never left my hand.)

Bowling is a ratings force on ABC for several reasons:

• During its four-month winter/spring tour, the bowlers are on during the same 3-to-4:30 P.M. Eastern time slot almost every Saturday. So, in an increasingly fractionalized sports TV viewing world, they're easy to find.

• It's an amazingly simple TV sport to watch. Two bowlers on two lanes; there's no hidden action beyond the camera. You could do the whole telecast with four cameras or so.

• The format in the stepladder TV finals rewards the viewer frequently. The top five bowlers from the week make the finals. No. 5 plays No. 4, with the winner playing No. 3, with that winner playing No. 2, with that winner playing the No. 1 qualifier for the championship. This means that every twenty minutes or so, another conflict is resolved, and viewers often latch on emotionally to a competitor trying to bowl his way up the stepladder.

Note: In 1993, ABC made a tragic adjustment to its time-honored bowling format. The network reduced the five-man TV finals to a four-man affair, with the winner of each week's tournament then taking on another bowler at the end of the telecast to determine the so-called "King of the Hill." This "King of the Hill" business is an anticlimactic, artificial nuisance. I'm hoping it's a one-year aberration. If it's not, if ABC insists on jamming this manufactured nondrama down our

throats again next season, I WILL HAVE TO CONSIDER SHIFT-
ING MY VIEWING ALLEGIANCE TO "AMERICAN GLADIA-
TORS." I hope all parties are abundantly clear on this issue, and
if I am forced to leave the bowlers behind, I just want Chris and
Bo to know there are no hard feelings.

Ah, Chris and Bo.

Since the ABC bowling show began in 1962, Chris Schenkel has been there. And since 1975, Nelson "Bo" Burton, Jr.,
has been by his side. They are the longest-running two-man
team in network sports. They are soft—you won't mistake
them for Jim Lampley and Johnny Miller—and they are forgiv-
ing and they are generous to all bowlers and all cities and all
tournament officials, but this is one time I say OK to all that
because it fits the tone of the telecast just fine.

ABC's bowling is the homiest, earthiest hour and a half in
sports. Each telecast has this comfortable, familiar feel to it,
starting with Schenkel's vanilla ice cream approach to announcing all the way to the sponsor's presentation of one of
those oversized checks to the winner. To Schenkel, every telecast is a paradise of pins. He's never met a bowling alley he
didn't like. And the man likes Toledo and Akron so much, I
can't believe he doesn't summer in either city.

Meanwhile, Burton—simply known as "Bo" to all bowlers—analyzes the lanes (lots of talk about oil concentration,
oil patterns and gutter-to-gutter oil), details the bowlers' vary-
ing techniques and, most important, acts as the de facto play-
by-play broadcaster by updating the viewer on where each
bowler stands in the match, particularly in the critical final
frames.

Bo also says things like, "Hit 'em thin and watch 'em spin"
and "Trust is a must or your game is a bust" and "Boy, oh boy,
Chris, did he bushwhack that rack" and, well, I just kind of love
it.

(Unbelievable fact: I can name more pro bowlers than I can U.S. presidents.)

(Unbelievable consequence: And people wonder why I have such a spotty social life?)

Key to this slice-of-Middle-America appeal are the bowlers and their families. The bowlers look like average Joes. The bowlers' wives look like someone you or I may have dated. (If I'm somehow insulting anyone here other than myself, I apologize.) In the era of million-dollar athletes in every sport, tournament purses in bowling are relatively modest and few bowlers top $100,000 in earnings *for a year.* This is one time in which showing athletes' families cheering them on seems appropriate, considering that most of them travel the country together in mobile homes.

Watching the bowlers again is like rediscovering the simplest childhood pleasure. (In fact, many of us who bowl on the sly are the same ones still eating Frosted Flakes.) And in these days when auto racers are no more than walking commercial billboards and viewers become jaded by the sheer volume of events, tuning in to ABC's bowling telecasts is like wandering into a small-town five-and-dime. It's a step back in the right direction.

That Stench
in the Air
Is All-Sports Radio

I was pushing eighty on the Pacific Coast Highway, the top popped down on my Jaguar XJR-S, with the ocean to my left, the mountains up ahead and California dreamin' all around me. Gripping the steering wheel with my tanned and muscular arms, I soaked up the warmth of the sun, the wind whipping through my thick and golden hair. I had my woman by my side, with her dark and haunting eyes radiating our deep and vibrant love. I felt alive and alert and athirst for all the wonders the open road could bring. And, at that moment on this endless summer's day, the only thing missing were good tunes, so I flipped on the radio looking for the Beach Boys or The Boss or maybe even some Juice Newton.

I got Stu in Torrance talking about a possible Eric Lindros trade.

Yes, it's all-sports radio, *and they're chatting up hockey in July!!!* I nearly drove into a coral reef.

For all you think-tankers searching for signs of malaise across the mainland, you need look no farther than your AM dial. All-sports radio, once just a small nuisance, has risen to cultural menace. Talk is cheap everywhere these days. The nasty trend began like most do—in New York, naturally—and has spread to at least a dozen cities in the past five years.

So on your car dial these days, all you usually get is schlock radio (Howard Stern) or jock radio (Howie in Teaneck).

It's all-whine all night on all-sports radio. All over America fans are mad, and Ross Perot's electronic town hall already is in session on the sporting airwaves. These folks whine and whine and whine—they're angry about player salaries and TV announcers and lousy management and bad coaching and shoddy umpiring and even poor groundskeeping.

Most of all, they're upset because THEIR TEAM IS LOSING.

These folks are never happy. Their teams don't win enough; when they do win, they don't win by enough. In town after town the question of the day is, "What is wrong with *our* team?" Lost on these radio rebels is a simple truth: Someone's gotta lose. Half of all teams have losing records at any given time, and, of course, only one team can win it all in any given season. No matter to Mitch in Rosemont and Vic in Rockville: WE WANT TITLES! OFF WITH THEIR HEADS!!!

You can't believe how many managers are fired after midnight on all-sports radio.

That's the worst aspect of all-sports radio: It creates a siege mentality among the sporting public. It's a feeding frenzy—first a couple of frustrated fans call in insisting that the local club make a move, then others follow frantically. Suddenly, there's a lynch mob gathering on the airwaves, and as the night wears on, the emotion grows. By early morning, a posse has gathered outside the victim's home. And very often, it's the "outspoken" talk-show host—acting reasonably irresponsibly in the name of higher ratings—who rouses the rabble and orchestrates the electronic execution.

The talk never stops.

At this very moment you can be assured that somewhere in America two sporting guys are crackling the airwaves with a discussion of good middle relievers in baseball. In fact, almost everyone still up at 3 A.M. these days can be divided into just two groups: those calling all-sports radio to vent their spleens and those calling the Home Shopping Network to order zirconium cuff links.

It's getting kind of scary out there; but at least we know these folks spend most of their time homebound, on the phone. Out of sight, out of their minds.

Who exactly are these people? This much I'll say: The next time there's a serial killer on the loose, homicide cops could do worse than tuning in to sports radio for likely suspects. (If sports radio existed fifteen years ago, Travis Bickle would've spent his downtime trying to smoke Billy Martin.)

Geez, whatever happened to Top 40?

Actually, like Top 40, sports radio plays the same talk over and over again.

Host: "Let's go to [your neighbor's name here] in [your hometown here]."

Caller: "The [your favorite team here] stink! They should fire [your home-team manager here]! How come [your team's biggest-name, most-overpaid star here] can't hit? I wish [team owner's name here] would sell the club! *We've got to make a trade!!!*"

All sports talk, indeed, always turns to trades. Every caller wants to make a deal. If Monty Hall is thinking TV comeback, he should start on sports radio. All they ever do on these shows is make trades; it's like a rehab center for Rotisserie League rejects.

Well, here's the deal I'm willing to make: I'll stop whining about jock radio if someone gets me some Toto cassettes for my tape deck.

Confessions of
a Closet Viewer

In the darkness that is my life, it can happen at midnight or at midday—I pull down the blinds, pull up in front of the television and take in various suspect shows that few in respectable or rational circles would acknowledge watching.

The fact is, there's a lot of sports programming I shouldn't touch with a 10-foot remote that I keep touching. And, because of the solid reputation I enjoy in the community, I've always been afraid to admit these viewing habits for fear of being socially ostracized.

Until now.

Here then, Confessions of a Closet Viewer:

• **"Bodies in Motion" (ESPN).** "Today we are going to work on the waist, triceps, biceps, aerobics, abdominals and concentrate on the buttocks!" Body by Jake, body by schmake; Gilad Janklowicz is my main man in motion. He doesn't just exercise, he exerts and exhausts and exhilarates. This guy's so healthy, he considers vitamins junk food. When he dies—that is, *if* he dies—he'll be doing sit-ups at the viewing.

Gilad is to workouts as Moses was to the Ten Commandments.

For thirty minutes daily, Gilad stays in motion, speaking rhythmically to the background music. Your TV screen sways along with him. He never stops, he never wavers, he never tires. He goes to commercial in motion, he comes out of commercial in motion. You can't turn the show off; it has a hypnotic effect, like watching a fish tank or a crackling fire.

"Let's do some serious abdominals!!!"

"Let's do eight more like this!!!"

"Let's do it better than ever, and this time you must keep the back flat!!!"

Let's clarify one point: Do I actually perform the workout? What are you, nuts? Gilad's outdoors in heavenly Hawaii, I'm indoors in Body Hell. I follow the program from my bed. (Because of an occasional guilt pang, I sometimes do roll over to my other side at mid-show.)

And I love when Gilad exhorts us, "C'mon, keep your stomach pulled in . . ." or "I want to see you drive those elbows to the knees. C'mon, guys, you have to do better!" LIKE HE CAN SEE US AT HOME CHEATING ON THE EXERCISE!!! And then, as the show is coming to a close, Gilad insists, "Keep going on your own through the break. Don't stop!"

Yeah, right, Gilad. Even Jack LaLanne's quaffing Yoo-Hoos by this point.

• **"NBA Inside Stuff" (NBC).** This show could be subtitled "Bodies in Motion." It celebrates beauty and power, youth and speed. It looks good, sounds good, feels good. It's the NBA's MTV, a sports-and-music fusion that's all splash and dash and flash.

Of course, there's no trace of the show fifteen minutes after you've seen it.

"Inside Stuff" is sort of like a stick of chewing gum—good while it lasts, forgotten when it's gone.

Michael Jordan, understandably, appears about every twenty-two seconds of the program.

The heart and soul of "Inside Stuff" is the slam-dunk segment called "Jam Session"—fast action and loud music, visually appetizing and spiritually unfulfilling.

"Inside Stuff" is cohosted by Ahmad Rashad (original name: Bobby Moore) and Willow Bay (original name: Cotton Fitzsimmons). They are very good at what they do; it's just hard to figure out exactly what that is. This much I'll give them: If you're having a dinner party, Ahmad and Willow are the folks you'd want greeting guests at the door. (Ahmad's the one with the earring.)

"It's the fastest half hour on television," Ahmad said at the end of one show. It is, and they even have a 24-second shot clock ticking down on the set. I just wish they'd use it. (You know, if Ahmad or Willow doesn't say something hip or cool before the clock expires, then neither can speak until the next commercial break.)

• **"Love Connection" (syndicated).** This show, of course, could also be subtitled "Bodies in Motion."

"The Dating Game" was too puritanical; "Studs" is too provocative. "Love Connection" achieves the perfect sociosexual balance: Give a little bit of information and leave a lot to the imagination.

Sure, a lot of you are saying, "This isn't a sports show."

Hah! A live studio audience lets out yelps at the racier parts like a raucous Big Ten crowd. The host acts as a referee between the dating parties. Each date has a pregame and postgame segment. There's a scoreboard—regarding which video contestant the audience thinks should be picked for a date—and there's a split screen. And if Chuck Woolery ever calls in sick, Pat O'Brien could host this baby in his sleep.

The only part of the show I don't like is when the date comes out from backstage and the couple hugs and embraces like they've known each other forever. THEY'VE HAD ONE DATE, FOR CRYING OUT LOUD! My God, I didn't even touch my ex-wife until a week or so before our divorce trial began.

You've got to love Chuck Woolery. (Jim Lange, Jim Schmange.) Chuck is fluent in body language. Chuck raises his eyebrows, Chuck rubs his forehead, Chuck appears bewildered, Chuck covers his face, Chuck gets that knowing look when he's sharing an embarrassing moment with us at home.

I like how Chuck leads each woman over to the couch; he greets her and, clasping her hands, brings her over gently. I like how Chuck shifts in his seat, from the woman on the couch next to him to looking at the man-on-the-screen backstage. I like when Chuck tells a couple after a disaster date, "Well, Don and Brenda, I'm sorry we didn't make a love connection for you." I like when Chuck says, "We'll be back in two and two," signifying the numbers with his fingers that the commercial break will last two minutes and two seconds.

And, of course, I like when Chuck ends the show by telling us, "Hope all your dates are good ones. Good night, everybody."

Chuck is The Man; Mark DeCarlo is just a body.

Besides, do you think I could ever get on "Studs"?

If the Price Is Right, I'm an NFL Pay-per-Viewer

I moved from Washington, D.C., to Los Angeles recently. This was seen as an act of insanity by many thoughtful people, but there were few problems and I adjusted well to the new environs. I liked the weather, I liked the food, I liked the lifestyle. Although I'd been a lifelong Washingtonian, southern California felt like a good fit for me. I even contemplated raising a family out here, that is, if I could ever find one.

I loved L.A.

Then the NFL season started.

I couldn't watch the Redskins anymore.

This was insane.

I wanted out in a New York minute.

I couldn't believe that, in all the time I spent contemplating the ramifications of a cross-country move, in all the thinking in regards to professional and personal and financial needs of mine, in all the planning for potential various contingencies, I never even considered the fact that I wouldn't be able to see every single Washington Redskins game from opening kickoff until final gun as I had since, oh, 1922 or so.

I mean, the only reason I even wake up at all autumn Sundays is to watch the Redskins. What was I going to do, sleep in for the rest of my life?

I had completely lost my mind.

And I had an apartment lease that ran well past the Super Bowl.

It was going to be a lost season, unless I acted quickly.

So I did what any other sporting American with an American sports car would've done: I drove around looking for satellite dishes. If a sports bar had the right china, I had a new home.

In less than thirty minutes I found what I was looking for, and shortly after got a glimpse of twenty-first-century sporting America.

Ladies and gentlemen, let me tell you—I have seen the future, and we are going to pay for it.

And, ladies and gentlemen, let me also tell you—I'll be first in line with my Visa card.

I found this splendid sports bar in Santa Monica. At the door each NFL Sunday, I handed over fifteen dollars. For my money, I was given four tickets; each ticket was good for a beverage, or I could exchange two tickets for breakfast or lunch. More important, for my money I gained access to twenty or so TV screens, with virtually every NFL game airing simultaneously somewhere within view.

On certain days in certain ways, America is a wonderful, wonderful place.

I would sit there, watching four or five games at once. It was both exhilarating and exhausting. If you try to take in too much, you can't take in anything at all. But once you get into a rhythm—and remember, I have trained for this my entire life at home by watching two TVs at the same time on big sporting weekends—you discover the ability to watch several games progress at once. I loved it when games appeared to be in sync—as one play ended in the Eagles game, another play would start in the Broncos game—as if all the contests were being choreographed by a single director, cuing each team when to snap the ball.

Of course, regardless of all the activity, I never lost sight of my primary goal—to catch every single play of the Redskins game.

Now, understandably, there are drawbacks.

For starters, you're watching these games with a couple hundred other people. Some of them tend to be loud and obnoxious. In particular:

(1) Many of them are drinking heavily.
(2) Many of them are smoking heavily.
(3) Many of them are from New York.

So you have a lot of people cheering a lot of different things and you have a lot of drunken chatter and you have a lot of smoke billowing around and you have these New Yorkers pretty much jeering everything from officials' calls to overdone cheeseburgers and, you know, in general it's just a real rowdy and raucous Sunday in the dark.

Don't get me wrong: I love it.

But there is a better way.

What we have here in Santa Monica—and in saloons across the country—is a crude form of pay-per-view. What we should have very, very soon is a better form of pay-per-view, the kind in which you don't have to leave your home.

Of course, I'm talking about NFL pay-per-view *from the comfort of your couch.*

NFL pay-per-view is a must. It is the most important social or cultural issue confronting this country today. We want it, and we want it now. The technology is in place, THEY COULD START IT TOMORROW. (I'd write my congressman right now, but coming from D.C., I never had a voting representative in Congress, and living now in L.A., I'm not even sure if I'm still on U.S. soil.)

It's simple. If you're a Cowboys fan in Seattle or a Browns fan in Miami or even, God forbid, say, a Patriots fan in Kansas City, for $9.95 or $19.95 you could punch up your hometown team's game most any Sunday. The key advantages here compared to the saloon system are obvious: a) no New Yorkers in your home and b) no lines to get into the bathroom.

And, under a plan I've been lobbying for since the late eighties, this baby could be incorporated easily within the structure of the current network TV contract:

Just as it is now, a regular schedule of games would remain on, say, NBC and CBS. Through pay-per-view, the NFL would allow viewers to substitute games within each network. This would protect NBC from losing viewers to CBS and vice versa. The NFL, the networks and cable systems would split the added pay-per-view revenues.

This pay-per-view plan satisfies all the key constituencies.

It satisfies the networks, which would be guaranteed fewer turnoffs by people who don't want to watch the game being televised in their region.

It satisfies the advertisers, who would have their national

spots seen regardless of which game is watched because viewers can only switch within each network.

It satisfies the league, which would reap higher rights fees and greater popularity.

It satisfies those viewers who have cable, pay-per-view and money to spend.

And if they do this soon enough, I won't even have to leave L.A., which would be a real hassle considering how bad traffic is going to the airport.

With Help,
You, Too, Can Survive
the Loss of a Remote

*E*ditor's note: *Several months before publication of this book, Norman Chad lost his wireless remote. To minimize the public-relations fallout, the TV industry—as well as readers and friends—were kept unaware of the development. But devastated by this profound change in his life, the controversial, oft-misunderstood TV columnist fell into a deep and dark psychological abyss, perhaps best detected by the erratic nature of his writing quality and shopping habits in recent weeks. Now, after three months of rehabilitation, Chad has been pronounced fully recovered by a team of media specialists. And here, at the request of these trained TV therapists, he goes public* *with his story for the first time and—to help others who one day might suffer a similar fate—describes the "Eight Stages of Remote Loss."*

It started like any other TV weekend. I woke up, I washed up. I wandered to the couch. I sat down. I reached for the remote. It wasn't there. I checked around—between the cushions of the couch, on the floor, in the onion dip. I had misplaced it before, but this time it was nowhere to be found.

It was gone.

You hear about this all the time, but you always think it's going to happen to the other guy.

I didn't know what to do. I could scan fifty channels a minute, fifty-five on weekends. Like millions of other Americans in recent years, I had never even touched my TV set. If I were standing six inches from the set and decided I wanted to watch television, I would walk around until I had found the remote. I wasn't even sure if the TV set had an on/off button. The remote was my lifeline to the wonderfully vast wasteland of images to which I was married.

Little did I know how long it would be before I would accept the fact that the remote was out of my life.

Through the help of TV doctors—plus discretionary use of those $2-a-minute 900 numbers and a brief tryst with a cable installer named Phoebe—I have persevered. It was tough eating TV dinners without TV. But stage by stage, I have come to terms with the loss of my remote:

- *Shock.* After mustering enough energy to turn on the TV, I just sat there. I was paralyzed. The phone rang, but I couldn't reach it. The doorbell chimed, but I couldn't answer it. I just sat there. As fate would have it, the last pre-remote channel I had been tuned to—gulp—was Nickelodeon. So Nick at Nite it was, hour after hour: "Get

Smart," "Bewitched," "Dobie Gillis," "The Patty Duke Show," "My Three Sons," "The Donna Reed Show," "Mr. Ed," "Lassie" and "Looney Tunes." I could not get up. It is possible, I was told subsequently by the medical people, that I did not even blink for more than sixteen hours.

- *Denial.* After the shock passed, I refused to concede that the remote was gone. Rather, I told myself, it was simply disguised. I got a Hershey bar from out of the kitchen and used it as the remote; the stations wouldn't change. Then I tried some personal-size Ivory soap; the stations wouldn't change. Finally, I started banging my hands together—I had bought several friends "The Clapper" in years past—but the stations wouldn't change. It was Nickelodeon, night after night. I believe "Inspector Gadget" was on when doctors finally made their way in through a loose bedroom window.

- *Depression.* You want to talk depression? I'll talk depression: insomnia, loss of appetite, a sharp sensation through my left (remote) hand, hallucinations of growing up with Mel Kiper, Jr. I hung my head so much, one of the medical team positioned the TV at my feet so I could watch "SportsCenter."

- *Anger.* I was mad, I was bitter, I was resentful. A good friend, Erica Coffey, phoned and told me to move on with my life, to "face up to the realities of the real world." Who the hell is she? I sent her a letter bomb, C.O.D. I wanted my remote back, not some useless bromides from a two-bit harlot.

- *Sadness.* The hurt set in. I felt like a lifeguard without a whistle. These were despondent, disconsolate, dismal days of despair. What's the word I'm looking for? Sadness, I guess.

- *Remorse.* I was filled with self-pity, a deep, torturing sense of guilt felt over a wrong I had done. If only I had been more careful with the remote, if only I had paid more attention to the remote, if only I had slept more often with the remote. You just can't take a remote for granted.

- *Loneliness.* I felt a profound sense of separation. Emptiness engulfed me. Erica Coffey phoned from her hospital bed to wish me well, but I was too forlorn to speak. I thumbed through mail-order catalogs, longingly gazing at the latest, hottest remotes on the market.

- *Acceptance.* Finally, during a tense early-morning session that verged on violence, Dr. Horace Steinkempf spoke for the entire eight-person medical team when he said, "Norman, you either accept this now, or we charge you for another week." I'm a reasonable man, and considering they were holding me down by my wrists and waist and blasting best-of-Bob Trumpy videotapes into my VCR, I saw the light.

I'm better today than I was yesterday, and I'll be better tomorrow than I am today. I've moved the coffee table to afford me a more direct route to the TV; I'm wearing ankle weights to give the 16-foot walk back and forth a healthful purpose. I like the idea of watching entire programs without switching channels, with the exception of the NBA on TNT.

And one day, deep in my heart, I know I'll have another remote.

In Ivy League,
Football Is Strictly
by the Book

I was clicking between the Southeastern Conference game of the week (on TBS) and the Notre Dame game of the week (on whichever broadcast carrier was the highest bidder that day) when I stumbled upon something quite odd-looking and seemingly out-of-place:

Ivy League football.

Eggheads gang-tackling eggheads! On live television!!!

I did the gutsy thing—I put down the clicker, picked up some stock listings and decided to be an Ivy League man for the day. First of all, unable to gain admission to an Ivy League school, I figured watching Ivy League football was the closest

I could get to those hallowed halls. Second, with the TV dial full of your Oklahomas and Miamis and Southern Cals, I figured it was nice to see *college* football, for a change.

The Ivy League's first national exposure in recent years came with a "Game of the Week" on PBS, a.k.a. "Masterpiece Football." Marty Glickman announced those games, and of course, there were no commercials. You half-expected to hear chamber music.

Subsequently, the Ivy League moved to ESPN and then, through a package of Cornell games, to SportsChannel—commercial cable networks that need the inventory so badly, they're even willing to put on bookworm football.

Turn on the Ivy League these days, and, despite the commercials, it still looks different from anything else on a football Saturday. It's nice to see a game where the stands are half-empty. In the bleachers, there are a lot of coats and ties. Most college stadiums divide the seating into student sections and alumni sections; at Ivy League games, it's divided into L. L. Bean and Burberry contingents.

Admittedly, I was a bit reluctant to tune in Ivy League football. After all, watching Columbia players break tackles is sort of like watching Clemson athletes go to class. What's the point?

The game I chose (on ESPN) was Brown at Cornell, with play-by-play broadcaster Wayne Larrivee and analyst Kevin Guthrie. (I was hoping to get George F. Will and Carl Sagan as sideline reporters, but, alas, I was disappointed.) Let's get one thing straight right now: Guthrie may be a Princeton man, but in the booth, he's just another ex-jock analyst who has graduated from the Bob Trumpy School of Public Speaking.

Larrivee—although he's a Big Ten guy—tried to adjust to being around actual institutions of higher learning. For instance, he once referred to a "judicious blitz." Another time, instead of describing a receiver catching a pass "out of bounds," he said the player was "out of real estate." You've got to play to your audience, so give Larrivee the benefit of the doubt.

It was nice to watch old-fashioned college football. No blimps. No spring practice. No scholarships. No redshirts. No freshmen.

Also, no speed.

It was like watching an entire game in slow motion. (Replays, for instance, could be shown at full speed.) The game would've had a better flow, I think, if the linemen didn't bring poli-sci books onto the field with them. When the quarterback barked signals, they were mathematical equations.

Hey, they might have been slow, but they also were smart.

I was extraordinarily impressed with these fellows' academic credentials. (Granted, I went to the University of Maryland, where the operative educational term is "parking tickets.") From the look of their majors, it appeared Ivy League players actually have classroom obligations.

Here's a sampling of their majors highlighted on the telecast: Brown's Mike Lenkaitis, organizational behavior and management; Jason Pankau, business economics; Rob Dumanois, public policy; Cornell's Tom Dutchyshyn, mechanical engineering; Paul Tully, business management; Scott Oliaro, nutritional sciences.

I've watched entire Alabama-Auburn games in which the only majors listed were "general studies," "American studies" and "undergraduate studies."

(To be fair, late in the game, two consecutive Cornell players listed were majoring in "hotel administration." That sounds suspiciously like Ohio State material. Let's be honest here: The only things you need to run a Ramada Inn are a degree of patience and an oversupply of towels.)

ESPN also ran a graphic reviewing some of the top graduates to come out of Brown and Cornell. It's hard to believe that the same school (Brown) produced John D. Rockefeller, Charles Evan Hughes, Nathanael West, Ted Turner—and Chris Berman.

The game seemed a bit sloppy. Punts looked like autumn leaves fluttering to the ground. Guthrie mentioned the "good football tradition at Brown," but it probably doesn't compare with the divorce-lawyer tradition at Brown. A dog—undoubtedly a purebred—ran onto the field in the third quarter. The field is named Schoellkopf Field, which is what a college field should be named.

The cheerleaders, by the way, looked like real people.

Cornell turned the game into a rout, winning 34–7. There were no incidents, like the game-ending melees that often plague other contests. This is not to say there wasn't trash-talking by players on both sides of the ball, but instead of "Your mother wears combat boots," it likely was along the lines of "Your father couldn't design a Stealth bomber."

It was an idyllic setting for a healthy dose of competition among true student-athletes.

Now, I hesitate to bring this up, because it detracts from my overall "Ivy League as Ideal Living" thesis, but there was one disturbing element to the proceedings.

It was the way Cornell reacted to scoring touchdowns.

Instead of the traditional "high-five" celebration—in which athletes gleefully slap each other's hands high above their heads—Big Red players would jump into the air and hit another part of their bodies against each other. There's really no other way to describe it than to call it a "high-butt," which should be fairly self-explanatory. I mean, you don't need an Ivy League education to figure that one out.

Let's Make a Deal
(But Be Careful
You Don't Get Zonked)

"**O**K, Jay Stewart, tell us a bit about today's chapter!!!"

"We've got people watching TV while eating, 7-Eleven patrons sounding off on female reporters and Ahmad Rashad showing up everywhere! All that and more, Monty, so take it away!!!"

Behind Door No. 1 . . .
TV Dinners on the Rise!!!

Ketchum Advertising of San Francisco commissioned a survey to explore American eating habits. Among the 500 respondents, 70 percent said they watched TV at least one night a week during their dinner, and 24 percent said they watched TV every night during dinner.

A couple of things to note here:

(1) People always lie regarding how much food they eat.

(2) People always lie regarding how much TV they watch.

So let me emphasize—I know people who often eat dinner twice a night, sitting down to the theme music to "Gilligan's Island" and again as the horn at a sports arena signals the start of the second half. In other words, those figures Ketchum obtained are low.

Consider this: At perhaps the most sacred American dinner, Thanksgiving, the carving of the turkey in many homes coincides with a late Lions rally that pulls them within two touchdowns.

The last time I had dinner without the TV on, I ordered my meal through a clown's mouth.

Bonus fact: At the Last Supper, Judas and Jesus had a tiff as to whether to watch the Nashville Network or SportsChannel Nazareth with dessert.

Anyhow, when I set the table these days for one of my many dinner parties, I place a fork on the left side of each plate and a remote on the right. Knives and napkins are the responsibility of each guest.

I believe the future of America is a combination microwave/TV in which one setting allows you to cook a Lean Cuisine lasagna entrée and condense Roy Firestone's "Up Close" ESPN show into a single serving.

Behind Door No. 2 . . .
Slurpee Set Says No to Women!!!

As part of a "sound off" series, 7-Eleven asked its customers one week: "Should women reporters be permitted inside men's locker rooms?" With more than 7.5 million votes cast, according to the convenience store, 50.2 percent answered no and 49.8 percent yes.

A couple of things to note here:

(1) Many of the people who "shop" at 7-Eleven—and I use that term loosely—are young, marauding males with a salt imbalance seeking to purchase between ten and seventy-five dollars' worth of junk food at three o'clock in the morning.

(2) To vote, consumers chose coffee or soft drink cups marked "yes" or "no." (This is not exactly the electoral process our Founding Fathers had in mind, but then again, this is not exactly the type of country our Founding Fathers had in mind, either.)

In other words, it's miraculous the vote was as close as it was.

(Incidentally, another recent 7-Eleven weekly "sound off" question was: "Will you marry for money?" Frankly, I think a more appropriate 7-Eleven customer inquiry would be: "Will you date this decade?")

In related news, I conducted my own informal survey at my local 7-Eleven regarding the question, "Should men reporters be permitted inside women's locker rooms?" The guy in front of me in line answered, "Why the fuck not?" and the guy behind me in line answered, "Why would women have locker rooms?"

Behind Door No. 3 . . .
Ahmad Rashad, Come On Down!!!

The following sightings occurred on "regular TV"—not sports TV, mind you—over a two-month period:

Ahmad Rashad cohosting VH-1's weekly "Top 21 Countdown" of music videos.

Lynn Swann hosting the NBC game show "To Tell the Truth."

Joe Garagiola cohosting NBC's "Today" show.

Terry Bradshaw cohosting CBS's New Year's Eve telecast from Times Square.

Dick Butkus appearing as a reporter on the syndicated tabloid news show "Inside Edition."

A couple of things to note here:

(1) Ex-jock sportscasting celebrities apparently are in demand in the entertainment end of the industry.

(2) Ahmad Rashad apparently has become the Arthur Godfrey of the nineties.

In other words, when Letterman retires, we can expect Len Dykstra or Manute Bol to replace him.

We'll get back to this Ahmad Rashad phenomenon in just a moment.

As far as ex-jocks becoming entertainment entities, it's time for the truth to come out. Many TV producers today are products of the rebellious sixties counterculture and, finally, the lifestyle of that era is taking its toll on Tinseltown's brain trust. Recreational choices made then are affecting decision-making processes now.

Yes, I'm talking drugs.

There's no way around it. How else to explain the bizarre dependence on ex-jocks on the part of game shows and comedy shows and even news shows? The executive producer these days of every other show, I'm sure, is Dr. Timothy Leary.

As for this Ahmad Rashad thing, it's now become easier to list those programs he has *not* appeared on than those he has: "Father Dowling Mysteries," "The Mod Squad," "Thoroughbred Digest" and "Love, American Style." I went into a Sears video center the other day and they had the "Ahmad Rashad Collection"—a line of TV sets that could be tuned only to shows he cohosts.

Ahmad Rashad is everywhere you are. He'll do weddings, bar mitzvahs, car wash openings. He's America's Cohost. If you don't have Ahmad Rashad, you may as well not even open your doors.

And now, the lovely Carol Merrill will show us what's behind the curtain . . .

Women Are Watching with Us!!!

The Arbitron Rating Co. details sports-viewing patterns in a guide called "A Review of the National Sports Scene." Generally, for all network sports events, nearly two-thirds of the audience is male. But as the number of sports TV hours in recent years has risen dramatically, women have come along for the added viewing.

Arbitron numbers indicate that almost as many women as men watch horse racing, that women watch the PGA Tour almost as regularly as men, that as many women watch ABC's pro bowlers as men. The NFL and the NBA also attract a healthy female viewership. (There is no concrete data on whether women are attracted to NBC's Paul Maguire.)

Conclusion: Although sports is still a male-dominated vehicle, women in the near future might find themselves part of an evolutionary tide that places them side by side with men— lying pitifully on the couch, slaves to Brent Musburger. Pass the pretzels and call it progress.

Believe It or Not, There Are a Few Good Things in Sports Television

By popular demand—well, actually, two people made a suggestion—in this chapter I am going to list my favorite things in sports television. (Understandably, this might be a shorter chapter than the rest.)

I think it is important in today's troubled times to accentuate the positive.

I know that many, many folks out there with whom I often speak—particularly if the conversation occurs immediately after any Norm Hitzges appearance on ESPN—have the perception that I don't like anything on sports television. This is not true. You cannot watch as much sports television as I do and not like it. (Incidentally, that was the basis of my ex-wife's closing argument in court as to why she had to divorce me; she said—and I quote—"You cannot live with somebody as much as I do and not love him. Thus, I must leave you.")

Marriage, schmarriage. Let's talk good TV! Here are a few of my favorite things in sports television:

NBC's Marv Albert, ABC's Al Michaels or CBS's Pat Summerall doing play-by-play of anything. Albert has the intonation, Michaels has the eloquence and Summerall has the economy.

The anticipation of a good "Monday Night Football" game on ABC.

John Madden.

The Goodyear blimp.

John Madden talking about blimps.

Sports reports on CNN's "Headline News" at twenty and fifty minutes past the hour—all scores, no fluff.

The Pro Bowlers Tour on ABC. If Bo Burton tells you the 7-10 split is virtually unmakable, then you know the 7-10 split is virtually unmakable.

Jerry McKinnis's "The Fishin' Hole" on ESPN. (Yeah, I bowl and I fish. And I watch bowling and fishing shows. What of it?)

Paul Maguire, when he's achingly funny on NBC NFL telecasts.

Greg and Terry on CBS's "The NFL Today."

That old, familiar theme music on ABC's Olympic telecasts, brought back by NBC for its 1992 Summer Games presentation.

Walking into a hotel room in a strange city late at night, dead tired, and turning on the set to get ESPN's "SportsCenter."

Waking up in a hotel room in a strange city noontime Sunday, dead tired, and turning on the set to get a full afternoon of NFL coverage.

Wandering into a hotel bar in a strange city in early evening, dead tired, and looking up at the set to see a Bulls-Knicks game in progress.

Pocket billiards on ESPN.

Fred Hickman and Nick Charles, hipping and hopping on CNN's "Sports Tonight."

Andres Cantor's demonstrative, elongated "Goooooooo-oooooaaall!!!" on Univision's soccer.

OK, OK, I'll admit it then—Keith Jackson's "Fuummmmmmmmmbble!!" is, indeed, entertaining.

Tom Durkin's nonpareil race-calling during NBC's Breeders' Cup.

The opening of ABC's "Wide World of Sports," including the never-grow-old, classic ski-jumping fall of Vinko Bogataj.

Gary McCord on CBS golf, Mary Carillo on CBS tennis.

Gary McCord's playful byplay with Ben Wright.

The music on "Monday Night Football" before they get to Hank Williams, Jr.

The tones that greet ESPN's twice-hourly sports updates.

Brent Musburger saying, "You're looking live . . ."

Charley Steiner, who does it the right way on ESPN's "SportsCenter." Also, John Saunders, Bob Ley, Keith Olbermann, Dan Patrick and Robin Roberts.

Plays of the month on "The George Michael Sports Machine." The man can really shift into overdrive when narrating fast-paced highlights packages.

ESPN's "Sunday Night Conversation" on "SportsCenter."

Bud Greenspan's unparalleled Olympic vision.

CBS's super slo-mo close-ups.

Towson State vs. Lehigh during NCAA Championship Week on ESPN.

Bob Costas, when he zeroes in on an interview subject on NBC.

Bob Costas, Brent Musburger, Bryant Gumbel or Jim Lampley—all born to run studio shows.

Eavesdropping on coaches' huddles or conversations with officials.

Remembering how Howard Cosell could fill up a screen like no one else.

Dick Schaap, adding a voice of reason to ABC and ESPN.

"Big Monday" on ESPN (usually with the sound down).

That NFL Films music.

Jack Whitaker's essays and caps on ABC.

The reverse-angle replay on "Monday Night Football."

ESPN's "NFL PrimeTime," even with Chris Berman.

The last five minutes of almost any NCAA basketball championship game.

Those in-car cameras on auto racing.

Alex Wallau's measured, honest commentary on ABC's boxing telecasts.

Watching any big-time title fight on pay-per-view.

Former NBC Sports executive producer Michael Weisman, anywhere near a production truck.

Radio bonus: Vin Scully, Ernie Harwell, Jack Buck or Jon Miller doing baseball in the dead of summer.

ESPN's "The Sports Reporters" and SportsChannel's "The Sports Writers on TV." (Hey, reasonably intelligent conversation among mostly aging, overweight, ink-stained wretches has always stimulated me.)

Beano Cook.

A night in which there is no hockey on.

There Are Three Kinds
of Stats:
Stats, Damned Stats
and *USA Today*

"Four out of five dentists surveyed prefer Trident sugarless gum for their patients who chew gum."
Now, that's a stat you can sink your teeth into. In fact, that's the first statistic I remember memorizing and believing as a kid—it had credibility (dentists being surveyed on something dental-related) and it had an overwhelming, one-sided conclusion (80 percent of dental experts agreed that a particular product was better).

Those were the good old days of statistics—when they were used rarely and reasonably.

Welcome to the New Age of Calculation, Enumeration and Overanalysis.

Bill James, come on down!!!
Norm Hitzges, come on down!!!
CompuBox, come on down!!!

Sports journalism has become a numbers game. On TV and radio, every game is littered with statistical debris; in newspapers and magazines, every story is filled with computable refuse.

The thinking is simple: If you have a stat, you have a story.

Game telecasts are cluttered with endless graphics backed up by endless babble from endless announcers hawking endless statistical truths. It's like trying to follow a Wall Street ticker: Too much volume is thrown at the viewer at once, rendering much of it meaningless.

It's an avalanche of numbers—sometimes contradictory—piling up on top of one another. There's a third-down efficiency in every yards-to-go situation, there's hitting average with runners on base and less than two out, there's free-throw percentage in a game's final five minutes with your team behind.

They are tales told by video, full of stats and figures, signifying nothing.

Baseball is the most natural stat disaster night in and night out—the game always has lent itself to interminable statistical review—but all sports have been invaded by mind-numbing numerical conjecture. During the 1993 NCAA basketball tournament, CBS kept trumpeting two undeniable truths—that when North Carolina was ahead at halftime it had not lost a game all season, and that when Michigan was ahead with five minutes left it had not lost a game all season. Well, North Carolina and Michigan met in the title game. And North Carolina led at the half, so CBS brought out that fancy 25–0 stat, and then Michigan led with five minutes left, so CBS marched out the Wolverines' unblemished 29–0 mark in that particular situation.

OH MY GOODNESS, THIS MEANT THAT NEITHER TEAM COULD LOSE THAT GAME ON THAT DAY.

What was the NCAA going to do?

What do these stats really mean, anyway? Of course a good team should have a very gaudy won-lost record when it leads with five minutes left—after all, that team is ahead, sometimes by a lot of points, and it's pretty darn late in the game. So what's the big deal about that stat?

(Here's a meaningful stat for you: Nobody gets out alive. I mean, *nobody*. That's ZERO percent. I'm sure Tim McCarver has a reason he could share with us.)

For years, ABC—on its "Monday Night Baseball" and "Monday Night Football" telecasts—had a knack of putting up the right stat at the right time. Nowadays, TV folks put up any stat at any time. And these numbers often linger on the screen over live action; it's like trying to watch the Playboy Channel through a scrambled picture.

The business of sports journalism is being overrun by the numbers people. It's an offshoot of the computer age, with an accountant's mind taking control of the production truck and the word processor. There's a reverence for numbers among these Roto League ledgerheads, and stats often are mistaken for the absolute truth.

All these numbers provide a lot of text without any context.

This slide-rule reporting also speaks to our shortening attention span—the only truth that counts is how quickly we can get it. Hey, everything can be quantified by numbers, so why not?

Two media institutions have emerged in the past decade to lead this numerical assault: ESPN, which operates as a 24-hour sports-and-stats emporium (always remember: Where there's excess, there's ESPN) and *USA Today,* which could reduce a nuclear holocaust to a pie chart. Both places have a lot of time and space to fill, so they roll out the big lists and big charts and big graphics and big diagrams and big box scores until that big garbage canister of small and insignificant numbers can hold no more. (When Thomas Jefferson said, "Were it left to me to decide whether we should have a government without newspapers, or newspapers without government, I should not hesitate a moment to prefer the latter," I guarantee you he had never seen *USA Today.*)

ESPN goes "inside the numbers" so much, you half-expect "SportsCenter" to hold lottery drawings before every commercial. If they ever cut open Chris Berman, they might find an abacus in there.

As for *USA Today,* those Gannett reporters have program keys for fractions. First there was painting-by-numbers, now there's writing-by-numbers. The old newsroom shout "Get me rewrite!" has been replaced by "Get me graphic art!" *USA Today* staffers don't get paid by the word, they get paid by the number.

And somewhere along the line—because stats have no soul and numbers can't tell all—the whole complex and difficult task of explaining truths and enlightening masses has become a secondary player in journalism's dizzying thirst for sports-by-the-numbers. There are a lot of stories out there falling into the cracks of calculators. I don't have any statistics to prove it, but I just know it.

On the other hand, I'm still chewing Trident.

Choices Are Clearer
in Black-and-White

In my parents' den sits a Panasonic 27-inch stereo color TV. It has the most penetrating picture I have ever seen, the most sensational sound I have ever heard. I often have imagined going into that room, turning on the TV and never turning it off; the newspaper obituary would report simply that I died of "sensory overexposure during a postseason basketball tournament televised on cable."

In my living room sits a General Electric 19-inch color TV. It, too, has a terrific picture. It, too, has an almost hypnotic quality that can lure me into a permanently prone position, with my eyes blinking idly at the flickering images deep into the night.

And in my bedroom sits a Samsung 12-inch black-and-white TV set. The picture is so-so. The sound is awful. And, you know, everything looks so small.

These days, it's my TV of choice.

More and more, I find myself watching everyday programs on the smallest screen in the house. Part of the idea, actually, is so I'll watch less and less.

The 12-inch TV has two big advantages—it's not hooked to cable and it has no remote. Thus, I have a relatively limited choice of programs and, equally as important, I cannot just sit back and switch from program to program. Yes, I actually get up and *change the channel myself* like everybody did when we all were kids and Bob Barker was still hosting "Truth or Consequences."

This is no small thing. After all, cable + remote = ex-wife in Florida.

For all of cable's promise, it's just a 24-hour video convenience store stocked with junk food. The remote ensures you don't even have to get up to shop. It can be mindless. Some people, with a bowl of peanuts next to them, will continuously sweep their hand from bowl to mouth to bowl without thinking about it, without even being hungry. Some viewers, with a remote in hand, will continuously sweep through fifty channels without really watching anything, without even wanting to watch.

With my 12-inch set, I have to make conscious decisions on what to watch. Sometimes—and this is a major statement around my apartment, where I'm on the viewing front lines—I just get up and turn the darn thing off.

I also like watching in black-and-white as a change of pace. Because almost everything I've watched for years is in color, seeing programs—particularly sporting events—in black-and-white is a different sensation. It also recalls for me a time when watching TV was more of an event.

I first thought of this recently while watching "The Wonder Years," the often brilliant ABC sitcom set in the late sixties and early seventies. During some episodes, Kevin Arnold and his family will gather around the TV for a good weekly show, and they'll always be watching in black-and-white. Then there was one episode in which Kevin's father was being pressured by the family to buy a color TV set; Kevin and his siblings would go to the appliance store and stand in front of the new sets, mesmerized by the wonder of color. The magnificent viewing possibilities seemed endless to them.

I'd like the possibilities to seem endless again.

To that end, I've started an informal new system of viewing that I now will share publicly for the first time. (Warning: This is going to sound stupid at first; well, frankly, this is probably going to sound stupid even after you think about it for a while, but hey, it's my life and my TVs and I'm not going to have some cable guy in a blue uniform tell me how to run things.) What I do is divide my viewing time depending on the nature of the program.

If it's just a "Cheers" rerun or a meaningless local college basketball game, I watch on the 12-inch black-and-white set.

If it's a pretty compelling sporting event, such as an enticing "Monday Night Football" matchup, I watch on the 19-inch color set.

And if it's something as big as the Super Bowl or a terrific pay-per-view title fight, I drive over and watch on my parents' 27-inch stereo color set. (It's to die for. Plus, if it's a pay-per-view telecast, I don't get the bill.)

This viewing system, which is as yet unnamed, takes care of many problems at once. At the bottom end, I watch on a TV without cable or remote and essentially limit my run-of-the-mill viewing. As I move toward the top end, I watch the most compelling events in the most compelling setting, re-creating more of that distinctive feeling that should come with the viewing experience. In addition, I get to see my parents, although they always want to talk to me more than I'd like. (They don't seem to grasp the purpose of commercial breaks, as far as I can tell.)

You, too, should experiment with this system. Of course, you probably need to buy a small black-and-white set as well as introduce yourself to my parents. (They're much nicer and not nearly as critical as I am. Really. But don't forget to wipe your shoes on the mat when you come in. Oh, Lord, can they yell.) By watching TV in the right dose in the right place, it just might feel right again.

The New Sports Bar:
Where the Games Are

When twenty-second-century historians write their cultural indictment of late twentieth-century America, they will wag their pens, undoubtedly, at sports, television and sports television viewers. Here was a society that elevated the playing field to ridiculous heights and sat back, sometimes to the exclusion of almost anything else, to watch the images flicker across the screen.

Increasingly, everyone in this new republic-by-remote retreated into the safety of their homes. Nobody went out anymore, except when the car took them from the driveway to the Safeway and back. And even groceries could be delivered, or better yet, pizza in thirty minutes or less. Of course, some folks still went to stadiums, but for every person in Joe Robbie or Mile High Stadium watching a Monday night football game, there were a thousand at home watching "Monday Night Football."

We came, we saw, we didn't get up off the couch.

And it was in this environment that entrepreneurial America, once again, seized the moment—or, more to the point, the money.

The sports bar was born.

The formula was simple: sporting event + big-screen TV + liquor license = commercial success.

To be sure, the casual sports bar always had been there. Even before television, there was the neighborhood saloon where neighborhood folks gathered to talk pennant races and title matches. Then, after television, there'd be the requisite TV set perched over the end of the bar, always on, always showing something even when something wasn't on.

Nowadays, though, the sports bar is The Sports Bar. Watering holes loudly sell themselves as sports bars, and countless establishments do big business when big games are on. They often go by names like Legends and Champions, they are big and boisterous, they are filled with large-screen TVs and sports memorabilia, they sell lots of liquor.

The Sports Bar is totally a television creation—for television, of television, by television. Yet what doesn't necessarily make sense is this: If the TV era has fostered a stay-home couch culture, how is it that people get up and go out to watch television?

To that end, sports bars market themselves as more than just bars that show sports. They often cultivate a charged atmosphere, a sort of stadium-extended mentality, right down to the cheering sections and interaction among fans. A game becomes an event, and a big event draws people out in much the manner of a smash first-run movie—people want to be there on opening night and want to be able to tell their friends they were.

Indeed, while VCRs and video stores have drawn more movie viewers into staying home, some folks, thankfully, still seek the excitement of going out and seeing a film on the big screen. Likewise, some people are willing to pay for a night out to see a game on TV that they could watch for free at home.

Moreover, some places have seized on seemingly divergent social phenomena—the sports scene and the singles scene—and cashed in on both. The sports bar/singles bar fusion is remarkable. Yet the cultures don't clash so much as they complement each other. In each case, there usually are the young and the restless in search of diversion, whether it be the thrill of a scintillating Final Four matchup or the thrill of the opposite sex. It creates some fascinating social dynamics, with TV talk and small talk drawing equal attention.

Make a bet, make a date.

Get a score, try to score.

Watch Ali dance, dance to Madonna.

It's the latest mating ritual of the nation. "The Dating Game" is best played At The Half.

And when you think of the overabundance of sports music videos in recent years and the insistence of sportscasters and sports producers on creating highlights packages to the beat of Top 40 sounds, you come to realize that people don't even think twice if a TV game in a bar is accompanied by a background blast of roll 'n' roll. The message is in the mixed media, the magic is in the mixed drinks.

Where do we go from here? Well, for starters, higher-resolution TV screens and state-of-the-art happy hours. There still will be the old sports bars—the dark, neighborhood dives with 19-inch sets—attracting an older, regular crowd. And now there will be the new Sports Bars—a bit too self-conscious, with memorabilia and door prizes and enough TV screens to fill a network production truck—attracting a younger, more transient crowd.

Most of us, though, will still be at home, and when they come and get us at the end, we'll be clutching potato chips in one hand and the channel switcher in the other, staring blankly into the emptiness of our sets. At least we won't have a bar tab to settle.

Position Wanted
(I Just Don't Know What)

It struck me the other day, somewhere between prime time and late night, that although I am the preeminent sports television critic of this generation, in the event that I decide to move on with my life at some point, I have nowhere to go.

Put another way, I seemingly am not qualified to do any other type of work.

In other words, I have no appreciable skills of any kind.

Bluntly speaking, I have absolutely no job prospects.

To be honest here, if I can't reach it from the couch, it's beyond my grasp.

How did I come to these conclusions?

Well, I typed up my résumé the other day. This is what it looked like:

AGE: Older than Doogie Howser, younger than the Golden Girls.

EDUCATION: American studies degree with a minor in soap opera.

EXPERIENCE: Own two TVs, two VCRs, four remotes.

FAVORITE FOOD: TV dinners.

WEIGHT: 165 by day, 172 by night.

MARITAL STATUS: Divorced (willing to remarry and divorce again, if necessary).

AVERAGE TV VIEWING PER DAY: 13½ hours, 16 on weekends.

FAVORITE SITCOMS OF ALL TIME: "All in the Family," "Cheers," "The Cosby Show," "The Dick Van Dyke Show," "The Honeymooners," "I Love Lucy," "The Mary Tyler Moore Show," "M*A*S*H," "Seinfeld," "Taxi" and "The Wonder Years."

LEAST FAVORITE SITCOMS OF ALL TIME: "Blansky's Beauties," "Bosom Buddies," "The Brady Bunch," "F Troop," "The Ghost and Mrs. Muir," "Good Sports," "Hello, Larry," "Joanie Loves Chachi," "My Mother the Car," "Three's Company" and any other John Ritter vehicles.

GOALS: To purchase a Smart Window TV set by Magnavox and to meet Justine Bateman.

HOBBIES: Nick at Nite.

REFERENCES: A. C. Nielsen; the NBC peacock; Hal, my cable installer.

So what conclusion do *you all* come to?

I can do next to nothing.

(When I was a kid, I wanted to be an otorhinolaryngologist; otorhinolaryngologists always get the women. But I hate when people sneeze around me.)

Sure, I can watch one program and tape another at the same time. I can program my VCR through my remote. I can order pay-per-view by speed-dialing. I can watch TV and make nonsensical notations on cereal box tops simultaneously. I can get pizza stains out of polyester shirts. However, none of these are marketable skills, unless you happen to be applying for work as Rudy Martzke's Boy Friday.

(Incidentally, do you all know who this Rudy Martzke is? He's the sports television columnist/press buffet scout for *USA Today,* a connect-a-dot newspaper that features a full-page weather map and detailed, four-paragraph stories on subjects ranging from nuclear disarmament to ketchup use in college dorms. The terminally pedestrian Martzke—this is a man who believes Judge Wapner sits on the Supreme Court, this is a man who considers Doritos a vegetable, this is a man who thinks *Roe* v. *Wade* is an upcoming pay-per-view fight—acts as a reporter, watchdog and critic over the sports TV and radio industries, that is, when he's not appearing himself on TV and radio every seventeen minutes or so. Whenever a story cries out for a look at The Big Picture, Martzke gives us Polaroid snapshots; if he were on hand to cover the Civil War, Martzke would've interviewed real estate agents on declining property values near key battle sites. If Rudy Martzke is the future of sports journalism in this country, then someone ought to sue the inventors of the printing press.)

How did I reach this static-filled, dead-end professional position?

True story: I was working as a homicide detective in El Paso in the late 1940s. There were just a few TV sets in town, mostly at bars. But one prominent local businessman had an RCA in his home. One night, though, a problem arose—he wanted to watch "Toast of the Town" while his wife wanted to watch "Gillette Calvacade of Sports."

They argued loudly. He finally stomped out, went to a nearby tavern and tried to persuade the proprietor to show "Toast of the Town" on his set. The bar owner agreed—for $3.95. All was well. Except that the husband had taken the only jar of cashews out of his home, and his wife was none too pleased. She came barging into the bar, shouting about what an insensitive lout he was. He politely asked her to wait for a commercial break. She persisted on badgering him. He took out a small pistol and shot her.

She was deader than CBS late night.

It was an open-and-shut case for me. Most TV cases are.

Postscript: The husband, convicted of murder, was paroled after six years and is now a top network programming executive. The bar owner is a pay-per-view mogul based in Los Angeles. I went from cop to critic in '53. The woman remains dead.

(For those of you believing that story—and I'm hoping, at this point, that we have a few takers—please proceed directly to the next chapter. For those of you who are a bit skeptical of the veracity of the preceding facts, oh, just keep your pants on and I'll have something else for you in a moment.)

How did I reach this static-filled, dead-end professional position?

In a little-publicized 1983 federal government study, 100 laboratory rats were exposed to four hours of sports television a day for six consecutive weeks. Half of the rats died by the end of the experimental period. The other half were assigned to daily newspapers as sports television critics.

You're looking at one of the proud survivors.

But it was a Pyrrhic victory at best, something akin to that of the folks in the nuclear-disaster film "The Day After" who might've envied the dead. Because once you are a sports television critic, you are absolutely nothing else.

In fact, sports television critics, it has been discovered, generally are spineless, a condition apparently exacerbated by years of lying indiscriminately on cheap couches. And sports television critics, it has been revealed, are lousy theatergoers, partly because they expect key scenes to be replayed in order to be understood properly. One historian recounts that during the fourth century A.D., when the Visigoths invaded the Roman Empire, ancestors of sports television critics refused to fight; rather, these video progenitors could be found on the high hills outside of Rome, with transitor radio-type devices, trying to pick up late-night chariot races from the west coast of Italy.

So here I am—Rudy Martkze with VCR Plus—and, believe you me, that ain't saying much. It's certainly not going to get me from my house to the White House.

Some of My Best Friends Are New Yorkers. I Just Hate Them.

I love New York; it's New York sports that I loathe. Anywhere you go in America, there's a New Yorker idling loudly next to you, and if he's not talking about the '69 Mets or the '73 Knicks or the '78 Yankees or the '86 Giants, he's telling you that the park or arena he's sitting in doesn't compare to *The Stadium* or *The Garden*.

Well, speaking for many of my sporting friends in Wheeling, West Virginia, and Lubbock, Texas, and Bakersfield, California, and all points in between, let me express a sentiment in a language that's pure, gripping Gothamese:

New York has wonderful food, theater and street life. It's got lousy sports. New Yorkers don't win or lose well; they gloat when they're on top and grumble when they're not. If you listen to talk radio there long enough, you can only conclude that every New Yorker either calls in to a sports show or hosts one.

So I find myself rooting against New York teams, particularly when I'm in New York. I figure if I can root against them there, I can root against them anywhere.

From the New York tabloids to the New York taverns, New York sports are overblown. Anytime the Yankees and the Mets win a couple of games, there is talk of a "Subway Series"—thusly named because fans supposedly could take the subway to all the games. Of course, it also might be called the "Oh My God I Hope That Crazed Man's Not Coming Over Here With That Sawed-Off Shotgun Series"—thusly named because of the wonderfully diverse and active underground culture in the city's mass transit system.

The hype carries over nationally. The Mets are picked to win their division just about every other year by innumerable national publications. When George Steinbrenner regained stewardship of the Yankees after his suspension, it was accorded the General-MacArthur-returns-home treatment. And when a New York team does actually win a title, trees in forests nationwide fear for their limbs, for there's always a glut of jock books on the grand season that was. (If Phil McConkey—Phil McConkey!—can put a book on the stands, the publishing industry might want to consider divesting.)

More galling is the long-held Big Apple sentiment, fueled

by the Manhattan media, that if it didn't happen in New York, then it didn't happen *at all*. Robin Yount will finish with 9,000 hits, but Bucky Dent's going to the Hall of Fame. (Speaking of which, New Yorkers complain loudest about three things— midtown traffic, lines at the bank and the fact that Phil Rizzuto hasn't made it to Cooperstown yet.) If Babe Ruth had played his career in Cleveland, John Goodman's only baseball movie would be *The Joe Pepitone Story*.

I'm still waiting for Kevin Maas to hit 60 home runs—for his career.

There's also this notion that New York has "the most so-phisticated fans in the world." Have you ever seen these people? The average New York fan is the "before" photo in a Jenny Craig ad, can go from zero to sixty and back to zero without braking and has a vocabulary roughly equivalent to that of a springer spaniel. "Hey, out of my way!" is the Gettysburg Address to most New Yorkers.

The most sophisticated fans in the world? I guess that's why they often cheer injuries of opposing players.

I love it when that elegant and urbane Knicks crowd expresses itself with the time-honored "BULLSHIT" chant; actually, I'm never sure if the locals are offended by the officiating or just trying to order food from a vendor. Similarly, when the Knicks go on a run, I'm never certain if New Yorkers are giving the home team a standing ovation or just trying to get up and escape the stench of their section.

Memo to Rangers fans: Call your parole officer.

I made my first trip to Yankee Stadium—excuse me, *The Stadium*—in 1980. The Yankees and Orioles were battling for first place, it was a beautiful summer night and the ball yard, indeed, seemed majestic. From our seats in the upper deck, everything felt right. Then, in the seventh or eighth inning, as a spiritual peace settled over this pastoral evening, I glanced over at an adjacent section. There was a man, with his back to the field, standing atop the last row of the stadium.

He was pissing into the parking lot below.

More than likely, this fella's got his own sports talk show by now.

I'll Take
World League Football
for $20

I walked into the Ramada Inn lounge at high noon Sunday. I like hotel bars for the big sports days. I particularly like Ramadas; they usually have that good mix of nuts at the bar. I sat down, took out a pack of cigarettes—I don't smoke, but it's an image thing with me—and sneezed twice to get the bartender's attention.

"Allergies?" he said as he reflexively wiped off the area in front of me with his bar rag.

"Nah, bad marriage," I muttered, reaching over for an ashtray and a pack of matches.

"So, what will it be for you today?" he said with a bright smile.

"It's going to be the World Bowl on ABC," I replied tersely.

"Sorry, partner," he said dispassionately, motioning with his head to the TV set.

I looked over and saw that the French Open was on.

"That's tennis on the TV," I offered, with incredulity.

"You looked like a man who can recognize tennis when he sees it," the barkeep cackled, with a smirk. "Sorry, pal, but the gentleman at the end of the bar wants to watch Agassi and Courier."

"Twenty dollars says we watch Brent," I said coolly, sliding a double sawbuck onto the lacquered mahogany bar.

And in one motion, the bartender took in the bill, picked up the remote and put on the football game.

Hey, this is America. I know how it works.

I ordered a Scotch, neat—I don't drink, but it's an image thing with me—and complimented myself on such a shrewd TV maneuver. Sure, I had to put out $20 to watch the World League of American Football, but pay-per-view's the future of this country, and I was just showing a little bit of vision.

"I wonder if they're going to have the HelmetCam today," the bartender said, slipping the booze in front of me. You give a guy some money, suddenly he's your best buddy.

So we made small talk for a while, and I told him the Monarchs would beat the Dragons because this Stan Gelbaugh was the Norman Esiason of the WLAF. I know this stuff. I'm a World League guy. Always have been, always will be. Spring football's where it's at in this country.

The pregame lasted twenty-five minutes. I asked the barkeep for the pay phone so I could flag my bookie—I don't bet, but it's an image thing with me—and after I faked a call and laid down a bogus $2,500 wager, I came back to watch the World Bowl—World Bowl I.

It was Brent Musburger and Dick Vermeil calling the

game—I'll tell you, I haven't seen Brent this pumped since the Little League World Series last summer—with Mark Jones and Jack Arute on the sidelines. (Anytime you've got Jack Arute, you *know* it's a big game.)

The lounge began to fill up, and some folks started grumbling as to why we weren't watching the fifth set of the French final.

"Hey, tell them to put their money where their mouth is," I groused to the bartender.

Vermeil, meanwhile, was in mid-autumn coachspeak cruise control: "seam patterns," "power rush," "pass offense mechanics," "rolled-up corner," "the stem of the route" and—my personal favorite—"negative turnover." Man, Vermeil was pumped, primed and prepped. He's always "in a zone" in that booth. He's so wired, he sets off the metal detector at every airport. Every time he yelled "Blitz!!!" I ducked.

I casually took notes on cocktail napkins; I had a job to do, after all, but I didn't want to call attention to myself.

Then, early in the second quarter, a classy-looking dame sat next to me. Looked like old money, maybe a Vassar education. I hit on her—I don't date, but it's an image thing with me—and she gave me her phone number, although I must admit I was not immediately familiar with the 777 area code.

The game dragged on. At one point, Barcelona coach Jack Bicknell barked out a play: "Beaver right, four hard naked slam."

I ordered a double Scotch, neat.

London dominated Barcelona—like the Super Bowl, the World Bowl was hard-pressed to match its hype—and the final was 21–0.

"They might give the NFL champs a good run for their money, eh?" the bartender said.

"I think you're right," I told him rather dishonestly, thinking *he* might give a bowl of oatmeal a good run for its money IQ-wise. "And I was just envisioning, anyway—one day the Super Bowl winner and the World Bowl winner will play, maybe in the Galaxy Bowl."

"You know," the bartender started, suddenly looking at me even more oddly than most people do, "I just realized who you are. You're the guy who writes about sports on TV."

"Right. . . . Can I get the check, please?"

I had to leave; my cover was shot. I had been recognized, and soon it would be a mob scene. I began walking out, shaking hands with well-meaning fellow viewers.

The barkeep shouted out: "Can I get your autograph?"

"Non, il faut que je parte maintenant," I answered—I don't speak French, but it's an image thing with me—and left in search of a Comfort Inn to watch the NBA finals.

My Years at
Sports Illustrated

My years at Sports Illustrated—January 1992 to January 1993, inclusive—were fruitful ones.

I got to write for the greatest sports magazine in America. I got to work with the greatest sports journalists in America. I got to be part of one of the greatest sports institutions in America. And I got to meet Judy, the Time-Life operator.

Gosh, what a set of knockers she had.

As you can see, I learned to fit in real well with the boys of Time Warner.

Let me recap.

I was hired by *Sports Illustrated* to write a weekly humor

column on sports and TV. This was not a good idea for either party. I was writing for a group of editors—very Caucasian and very male—who were pretty well educated, pretty well insulated, pretty darn middle-aged and, to borrow a line from *Good Morning, Vietnam,* pretty much more in dire need of a blow job than any white men in history.

I realized our aesthetics were clashing when my columns began being returned to me quicker than it takes a Time Warner editor to deny sexual harassment charges. (Note: For the record, during my fifty-plus-week stay at Sports Illustrated, I had twenty-six columns published and ten columns killed. Now, twenty-six for thirty-six is a good day if you're an NFL quarterback, but if you're a sports columnist or air-traffic controller, twenty-six for thirty-six is a signal to find another line of work.)

In its early years, *Sports Illustrated* was a literate leader in sports coverage. This was a magazine that published William Faulkner on the Kentucky Derby, a magazine that excerpted E. L. Doctorow's *Ragtime,* a magazine with a breadth of vision. And in the years I was introduced to it as a youthful reader—in the 1960s and '70s—there were revelations in the magnificent storytelling of Frank Deford and Mark Kram and Jack Olsen, in the hilarious genius of Dan Jenkins and Roy Blount, Jr.

By the time I went to work for *Sports Illustrated,* it was like going to work for a television outfit. That's what *SI* has become—a network whose pictures don't move. *SI* is as shrill as Dick Vitale, as slick as Pat O'Brien, as shallow as Chris Berman. It's a magazine that perpetually asks the dumb question. And, because it is part of Time Warner—which owns approximately 87 percent of the free world—*SI* is not so much a journalistic enterprise as it is a marketing strategy.

In the old days, a reader would be compelled to open up the magazine each week and discover a fascinating world of words and pictures. Now you get the magazine just so you can receive a free video in the mail.

Of course, some guys also like that annual fashion layout they do.

(Note: *Sports Illustrated* has an interesting policy toward women: 1. We put them on the cover at least once a year for the swimsuit issue; 2. We sleep with them on occasion; 3. We hire them on occasion, and then, if at all possible, we sleep with them after we hire them, for it can help down the road with key personnel decisions.)

In the days when *Sports Illustrated* set the tone for intelligent sports coverage, everything smart and savvy trickled down from *SI*. Now, mediocrity trickles up; *SI* follows the beat set by newspapers and television. In the age of ESPN, *SI* is carefully programmed each week, with little risk-taking. *SI*, once enterprising and literate and full of perspective, is just full of charts and other statistical debris now. It's the stuff of Rotisserie League.

Still, despite the fact that *SI* has gone from the high road to the lowest common denominator, the folks at the Time-Life Building in New York still think *SI* is The Show. Sure, they have the big cowboy hats, but they don't have any cattle; it's all bullshit and no bulls.

(Note: So how could *SI* fall so far so fast? Well, they took one of the worst writers in the annals of the publication—a guy known as "America's Guest" because of his unabashed free-loading, a guy who was a *hockey writer,* for crying out loud, a guy who if you took all the highlights of his published works you couldn't fill a matchbook cover—and they made him heir to Henry Luce. I don't want to name him—I fear the recriminations—but I'll tell you they made him managing editor and even publisher of *SI,* for a while. OK, it's Mark Mulvoy. There, I said it. I'll say it again: It's Mark Mulvoy. What's he going to do, make sure I don't get that staff position at *Entertainment Weekly* I've wanted so badly?)

In fact, when you think of *Sports Illustrated* these days, you think of the videos: Michael Jordan soaring; *The Best of Magic; NFL Bloopers;* Super Bowl highlights. In those relentless TV ads, the magazine doesn't even try to sell itself, it just sells the videos. The writing doesn't matter much anymore, even though it often is outstanding, for the articles are no more than filler between the photos and advertisements. Nobody pushes the envelope at *SI* these days, particularly since there might be ad money in that envelope.

Therein lies a key problem to the *Sports Illustrated* of the nineties: It is firmly part of the institutional, corporate nature of big-money sports. Heck, *SI*'s in bed with so many people, the magazine is converting offices into guest rooms. Chris Berman—Chris Berman!!!—is a sacred cow to *SI.* Why not? ESPN advertises weekly. (When I did submit a critical Berman column, Mulvoy killed it, then ran a lapdog feature several weeks later that all but declared ESPN's "SportsCenter" the greatest invention since the motorized golf cart.)

Publications often speak of the division between church and state—the editorial and business ends of the operation—as a sacred truth. At *Sports Illustrated,* there is no clash between the two entities. Editors with nice salaries, cushy futures and short workweeks act as church *and* state; they eliminate (read: edit out) any potential conflicts of business interests before any business interests can cry foul.

SI thinks "advertiser first," a.k.a. Build It According to Dealer Specification and They Shall Come with Large Satchels of Cash. At some point, Time Warner forgot the usual sequence: people are drawn to magazines for information and entertainment, then advertisers follow in order to reach all those people. Time Warner has reversed the process—letting ad interests often set the agenda—and, along the way, turned many of its articles into no more than marketing fodder.

I swear, it's those damn videos that keep the whole company afloat.

Example Number 1 of *SI*'s Business Bloat:

In my sole meeting with *SI* managing editor Mark Mulvoy—who, journalistically speaking, makes Mel Kiper, Jr., look like Edward R. Murrow—he explained why he was upset with my Super Bowl column months earlier. If he had been managing editor at the time, he said, he would've removed the negative, joking references I made about Pepsi and Toyota, who, by the way, are *SI* advertisers. (I had written, "With all due respect to that Pepsi miniseries: Gentlemen, I *don't* gotta have it," and "Mike Ditka for Toyota? Whoa! Mr. America, Mr. Heartland, Mr. Let's Kick Some Iraqi Butt, what's the deal? I thought I saw the Bears late in the season taking their shoes off before huddling. Is that an all-you-can-eat teriyaki buffet at Ditka's restaurant? I guess even Da Biggest Bear has his price, albeit in yen.") Mulvoy said he wanted to put a stop to *SI* writers' "cheap-shot one-liners." (He called these one-liners "Curryisms," a reference to out-of-favor, soon-to-be-out-of-*SI* senior writer Curry Kirkpatrick.) Mulvoy then stated: "I'm not going to allow one-liners in any way to interfere with *SI* business." He said it would be one thing if the magazine did a whole "enterprise" piece on, say, Nike and its shoe empire, but it was another thing if I "sideswiped" Nike in a column about something else. "I will not allow that at all," he said. I believed him; after all, he had a pretty big office and I figured he must have some clout around the company.

Example Number 2 of *SI*'s Business Bloat:

Shortly after I began writing for the magazine, it prepared a "Letter from the Managing Editor" about me for publication. Franz Lidz, the *SI* staffer who was writing the piece, called to let me know about one problem: In response to a question, I had told him that I like to drink Rolling Rock; however, he said, some "higher-ups" would prefer if I could mention another beer. For instance, Lidz said, it would be good to mention an Anheuser-Busch brand, being that Anheuser-Busch was an *SI* advertiser. I told him, "Yeah, well, but I don't drink Budweiser or Michelob. I usually buy Rolling Rock." Lidz said he would "write around it." And that he did. In the "Letter from the Managing Editor" that appeared in the February 10, 1992, issue, the sentence that originally had begun: "His current likes run from poker to Rolling Rock," was changed to "His current likes run from poker to the beers of Latrobe, Pa." I tell you, those boys at *SI* sure are swift with the keyboard.

Hell, I shouldn't complain about the magazine so much. I got a nice severance package when I left—one month's pay and a sneaker phone.

They Said It.
I Comment on It.

"Senator, don't always believe what you see on television."

—Dan Quayle to Albert Gore during the 1992 vice presidential debate

Heck, maybe you can't believe what you see on television, but you can always believe what you *hear* on television. That is, what with the current technology and everything, if somebody says something incredibly stupid, you can be certain of it—I mean absolutely beyond-a-shadow-of-a-doubt positive that the person said what he said—by simply having your VCR conveniently recording at that precise moment.

In my home, the VCR runs twenty-four hours a day.

Thus, over the years, I have been able to preserve many, many questionable statements and amusing dialogues among broadcasters, jocks and ex-jocks. (You may notice a lot of statements and dialogue from bowling telecasts, largely because I watch a lot of bowling, largely because I have the social life of an automatic pinsetter.) I am here to present some of those questionable and amusing comments to you, and, of course, to comment freely on those comments myself. I allow myself that indulgence—the right to comment freely—because if someone is diligent enough to record around the clock and rewind the tape to the right spot and write down the ridiculous remarks, then that someone should be allowed to say what he wants, particularly in his own book. Let's roll the tape:

- Just before giving his "bowling tip of the week" on ABC—what you should carry in your bowling bag—Nelson Burton, Jr., made the following comment regarding the Yorktown Lanes in Parma Heights, Ohio: "It's a very lubricious condition out there today."

    Say what you will, but "lubricious" is in the dictionary. Bo knows oil.

- When Florida State's Douglas Edwards was felled by stomach cramps during the FSU-Indiana NCAA tournament game, basketball analyst Bill Walton said: "Get him in the locker room, stick something down his throat, get him to puke it up and play some ball."

    Better yet, let's get Big Bill into the production truck, stick something down *his* throat and don't take it out until the broadcast is over.

- Dan Hampton on "NFL Live" to Bob Costas: "Remember this, Bob—[the Dolphins] are 2–6 in games . . . played where it's under twenty-eight degrees."

    But I understand they've never lost on the same day as a solar eclipse.

- When NBC lost the picture during its Orange Bowl telecast, studio host Gayle Gardner remarked to studio analyst Paul Maguire: "I understand we have lost the NBC feed and we are now taking the Japanese feed. Paul, maybe you can help us with that."

  I'm a big Paul Maguire guy, but if he starts translating Japanese over a national network, we could be looking at Pearl Harbor II within twenty-four hours.

- After hosting a charity "Family Feud" with the Philadelphia 76ers, Ahmad Rashad commented during "NBA Inside Stuff": "You know, I had a lot of fun hosting that 'Family Feud.' It was probably one of the highlights of my broadcasting career."

  Of course, the other highlight was being sideline reporter for the "Isuzu Quarterback Challenge."

- On ESPN's trivia game show, "The Dream League," after the George Atkinson–led team had beaten the Jim Plunkett–led team, 400–0, host John Naber ended the program by consoling Plunkett, "The game was a lot closer than the score might indicate."

  I repeat: The final score was FOUR HUNDRED TO NOTHING. Some of you may recall Naber working the '92 Winter Olympics for TNT at Albertville; it didn't exactly conjure up memories of Jim McKay at Grenoble. FOUR HUNDRED TO NOTHING!!!!!!

- Bob Costas, just before the Olympic flame was lit at the Barcelona Games: "I do not believe we enter the area of overstatement to say that the entire panorama of this Olympic stadium right now is among the most memorable and breathtaking scenes I have ever seen in the context of sport."

Hey, Bobby, how 'bout the opening game of the Spirits-Colonels ABA playoff series in '75?

- At the U.S. Hot Rod Mud and Monster Truck Racing Super Challenge on NBC, announcer Bret Kepner said: "The phenomenon of monster truck racing has definitely taken the country by storm."

Exactly which country might that be, Bret?

- Talking about poor practice facilities near Barcelona for the Orlando Thunder, ABC's World League football analyst, Dick Vermeil, said: "To make matters worse, much worse, really—[there was a] swimming pool, vacation area, females, sunbathing, topless . . . It was a distraction."

Geez, I would've thought Vermeil running wind sprints from noon to midnight daily might've been even more of a distraction.

- ABC often wires pro bowlers for sound, but many bowlers on tour make very few sounds. Such was not the case with David Ozio. At the PBA National Championship, Ozio frequently encouraged his 16-pound ball verbally after releasing it. A favorite was: "All right, baby doll—hook, hook, hook! Yeah!!"

Romancing the ball is common in bowling. I often call my ball "sweet thing" and occasionally shout out, "Hit the pocket or don't come back, you no-good, low-rent, two-bit harlot."

- Tim McCarver, explaining why Doug Drabek's low pitches make it difficult for catcher Mike LaValliere to throw out would-be stealers: "The best balls to throw are those around the shoulders because, obviously, that's where his arms are."

Similarly, the best place to tell McCarver to shut up is near his head, because that's where his ears are.

- Tim McCarver: "Sometimes a base hit is the result of a good pitch."

  Sometimes a needless comment is the result of a bad analyst.

- Sean McDonough, referring to Pirates knuckleball pitcher Tim Wakefield: "His slowest pitch tonight has been fifty-four miles per hour."

  Tim McCarver, in response: "That's one mile per hour below the speed limit."

  Dare I say it—Timmy McCarver, Traffic Reporter?

- Tim McCarver, during Braves-Blue Jays World Series: "This is an interesting little chess game these managers are playing."

  John Dockery, before a Stanford-Notre Dame football game featuring coaches Bill Walsh and Lou Holtz: "What we have here today is a chess match in cleats."

  How come they don't actually play chess matches in cleats? And how come before chess matches, the analyst never says: "What we have here today is a football game in loafers."

- Lynn Swann, after Southern Cal quarterback Rob Johnson is tackled by Oklahoma: "That's a coaching-design tackle."

  Dan Dierdorf, after the Kansas City Chiefs' Dale Carter returns a punt along the sidelines: "That's good sideline management by Carter."

  What with all this cerebral sideline management and cerebral coaching-design tackling, it's actually somewhat of a surprise that more football players and coaches *don't* take up chess.

- Tim McCarver: "Children have a way of getting to the point."

  God, if McCarver were only a child.

- Pat Summerall, prior to a Redskins-Eagles game: "When the Redskins and Eagles meet, the game is usually won or lost in a place they call 'the trenches.' "

  It seems that every football field in America has these "trenches." Where the hell is George Toma?

- Charlie Jones, as we watch replay of Summer Sanders celebrating gold medal in 200-meter butterfly at Summer Olympics: "You've gotta love it!!! It doesn't get any better than this!!!"

  Charlie Jones, as Buffalo Bills cut 35–3 Houston Oilers lead to 35–31 en route to 41–38 overtime playoff victory: "You've gotta love it!!!"

  Charlie Jones, while hosting highlights package of Mazda LPGA Championship as we watch winner Betsy King high-fiving the gallery: "It doesn't get any better than this!!!"

  That is *one happy* broadcaster.

- Mike Fratello, during Game 7 of Knicks-Bulls NBA playoff series: "Loose balls may be in the end the difference in this game."

  And, you know, sometimes it's foul shots and sometimes it's rebounding and sometimes it's turnovers and sometimes it's who wants it worse and, of course, I guess you could say that sometimes it's loose balls.

- Exchange between John Saunders and guest analyst Sam Wyche before Chiefs-Chargers NFL playoff game:

Saunders: "So who's going to win?"

Wyche: "I think it's going to be about a 24–21 game."

Saunders: "For who?"

Wyche: "Twenty-four's gonna win."

I'm sure when the folks at TNT Sports hear this exchange, Sam Wyche will have a studio job wrapped up.

• Sean McDonough's opening for Game 1 of the National League Championship Series: "Autumn—nature's annual ritual expressed to the quiet explosion of colors. The foreshadowing of change to cool fall breezes. And yet, there is something familiar about this time of year, something comforting and distinctly American. [Roar of crowd is heard.] But nature isn't alone in its tribute to fall, for each October our national pastime spans the generations in a colorful and dramatic tradition of its own. Baseball in the fall. Like harvests in the heartland, it nourishes our inner soul. We'd be empty without it. Like a cool October breeze, we expect it. It is as inevitable as a fallen leaf. So put on your favorite sweater, America, it's time to play ball."

Just show us the game and leave the poetry to Bard College cocktail parties. JUST PLAY BALL, for crying out loud.

• Chris Schenkel, at outset of Firestone Tournament of Champions bowling telecast: "One thing about bowling: It's never rained out, because it's an indoor sport."

He was serious.

• O. J. Simpson on "NFL Live": "You know, one of the nice things about this job is you get to meet a lot of nice people . . ."

You know, Juice, one of the nice things about *this* job is that I get to keep a clicker nearby at all times.

- Marv Albert, before the NHL All-Star Game: "If hockey has a holy place, it is surely here—the Montreal Forum."

  I don't think hockey has a holy place, but if it does, I think it's surely a dental clinic somewhere.

- Nelson Burton, Jr., as brand-new father John Mazza wins match during True Value Open bowling: "Hey, Chris Schenkel, those new young daddies are tough to beat. You put the determination, the talent of a Mazza and put a new baby in his arms and look out."

  I hope at least he puts the baby down before he bowls.

- Magic Johnson, discussing Shaquille O'Neal's size-20 shoes with Bob Costas: "A big man usually has a big foot."

  Sure, that's a relatively stupid comment, but at least he didn't explain why a big man usually has a big foot, as Tim McCarver would have.

- Peter Vecsey, discussing Cotton Fitzsimmons stepping down as coach of the Phoenix Suns with "NBA Showtime" host Bob Costas: "Listen, he's been there four years, Bob. I've always felt that you should change wives and studio hosts every four years."

  When you think about it, then, I was actually ahead of the curve when my ex-wife left me after three and a half years.

- Pam, a thirty-four-year-old customer service rep, telling Chuck Woolery on "Love Connection" why she got divorced: "You marry a couch potato. He stays on the couch, he becomes a potato and eventually you become a potato right next to him and you're watching your life disappear. You're watching TV and everybody on TV is having fun and you're just sitting there."

This is exactly the type of mentality I had to put up with for three and a half years.

- Chris Schenkel had the following exchange at the end of bowling's Oregon Open with winner Mark Baker:

    Schenkel: "What are your plans now, Mark?"

    Baker: "A matter of fact, I've really got just two goals right now: I want to win next week with my partner Dave Husted and have a child real soon. It's kind of hard to get my wife pregnant by UPS."

    Schenkel: "A lot of common sense there."

    And don't I know it—I tried the UPS route. It doesn't work.

- "A personal note, if you will," Frank Gifford began, as he announced—during "Wide World of Sports"—the birth of his son Cody.

    Usually, I believe correct protocol calls for the parents to simply send out announcements in the mail. But I wouldn't know, being that my ex-wife flew the coop after three and a half years and before all my UPS deliveries had reached her.

- Jay Randolph, at outset of Olympic TripleCast White Channel coverage of equestrian at 5 A.M. ET: "And we have eighteen teams competing, eighty-two riders. You're going to see a great majority of them in better-than-five-plus hours of coverage."

    Actually, Jay—nothing personal—but NO I'M NOT.

- Comparing CBS Sports executive producer Ted Shaker and NBC Sports executive producer Terry O'Neil, Brent Musburger told Bob Costas on "Later": "There's no comparison. Shaker's not a line producer. He's a corporate politician. He couldn't go in and produce a Pop Warner football game."

Well, Brent should know, being that he's the guy these days who announces Little League baseball.

• As fans in London were celebrating the London Monarchs' 21–0 victory over the Barcelona Dragons in the World Bowl, Brent Musburger and Dick Vermeil had this exchange:

Vermeil: "The pubs will be alive tonight. . . . Do you think they'll stay open after eleven?"

Musburger: "I plan on finding out."

Vermeil: "So what else is new?"

I'll tell you what else is new: Brent used to do the *Super* Bowl, not the World Bowl, and Brent used to hobnob at the *Big League* World Series, not the Little League World Series.

• After fighting well in losing to Evander Holyfield on HBO, Bert Cooper told HBO's Larry Merchant—who had asked him if this bout put him on a different career track—"No more ESPN fights." He paused, then said it again: "No more ESPN fights." He said it four times.

I guess he's not an Al Bernstein fan. (I guess he's also not a savvy prognosticator of his own future—he *did* fight again on ESPN.)

• Billy Packer, in the final minute of regulation of Duke's 88–85 overtime victory over Michigan in the first month of the college basketball season, exclaimed: "Who said that regular season doesn't mean anything?"

I'm going to say this one time and one time only, Billy: Regular season doesn't mean anything.

- Nick Charles, at the opening of TNT's last day of Winter Games telecasts from Albertville: "And welcome to the final five hours of Olympic coverage on TNT . . ."

  Further indication that there is a God, and He is a cable subscriber.

- During the French Open, ESPN's Mary Carillo asked tennis ingenue Jennifer Capriati what was the goofiest question she's ever fielded. Capriati said it was, "What does your room look like?" Carillo then responded, "That's funny. Let me ask you something about your room. Do you have, like, tennis posters up and stuff, or is it a real girlie room?"

  Because inquiring minds want to know.

- When asked during a phone interview on CNBC's "Talk Live" what he enjoyed these days on sports television, Jimmy the Greek replied: "You know who I like? The boy who comes on ESPN at six-thirty at night. Greenberg, is that his name?"

  Actually, it's Firestone, as in Roy Firestone, and actually, I don't like him. (Here's an all-time Firestone moment: At the end of his annual Father's Day program, in which his dad, Barnard, always appears, Sweet Baby Roy—straddling the stool—sang James Taylor's "Daddy's Baby" while showing home movies and still photos of newborn son Andrew. I hope the Smithsonian has a tape of that baby.)

- During coverage of the "Bowling Shootout" on NBC, this was the exchange between Jay Randolph and Gayle Gardner as Randolph threw the telecast back to Gardner in the studio:

  Randolph: "Time now to go to New York [for] 'Prudential Update.' Here's the gorgeous redhead, Gayle Gardner."

Gardner: "Thank you, Jay, you bowling maven, you."

In the era of routine sexual harassment suits, one must admire Gardner for disposing of this particular matter so discreetly and effectively.

- Before the French Open final between Monica Seles and Arantxa Sanchez Vicario, Bud Collins offered: "I picked Moanin' Monica a long time ago. She shows you can grunt and be feminine."

Incidentally, who winds up Bud Collins before telecasts? He makes the Energizer bunny look listless.

- During an Indiana-Boston NBA playoff game, Ahmad Rashad spoke briefly with Ad Smits, father of the Pacers' Danish-born Rik Smits. Language wasn't too bad a barrier until conversation's end:

Rashad: "Good luck. I hope you stay around for a long time and watch him go all the way."

Ad Smits (after long pause): "What do you mean, 'watch him go all the way'?"

Rashad: "If they win the championship, he goes all the way."

Ad Smits: "Oh."

At which time play-by-play broadcaster Tom Hammond remarked to analyst Ron Rothstein: "Ron, you know, I understood Ad perfectly. It's Ahmad that I had difficulty with."

Hey, I've been saying that for years.

- Upon signing a one-year minor league contract with the Atlanta Braves organization, Deion Sanders explained: "I want to be on TBS or whatever it is."

As you grow older, your goals in life become a bit more pedestrian.

- After Robert Lawrence won bowling's True Value Open, Chris Schenkel asked the champion's wife, Sherri, about the fact that Lawrence had looked like he had a chance to roll a perfect game. Sherri Lawrence looked over at Schenkel and replied, "Where's the money?"

  In other words, let's just cut to the chase, Chris, and hand over the check already.

- The Cincinnati Reds were upset by a CBS decision that only starters got introduced before Game 1 of the World Series. Pitcher Norm Charlton said: "I guess five minutes of commercials is more important to them than giving recognition to each individual player."

  And, you know, Norm, buddy, it ain't even a close call for them.

- The syndicated talk/horror show "Geraldo" discussed the issue of female reporters in the locker room, and here was host Geraldo Rivera's hook-'em-in hysteria to open the show: "How would you feel if it was part of your job to interview famous members of the opposite sex who happen to be in the nude? Well, that's what these ladies do every day. They are all top-rated sports reporters, and believe me, just name any famous ball player and these ladies have seen him in various stages of undress."

  Next week, Geraldo talks to top female executives who go braless to Friday staff meetings!!!

- Three months after finishing a nine-year run as anchor of NBC's "NFL Live" pregame show, Bob Costas told guest Paula Poundstone on his "Later" program: "Football is a really stupid sport."

  Oh, so *now* we find out.

- When ABC asked David Ozio his plans after bowling, he said: "I hope that someday in the future when I start to drift out of bowling . . . I would like to pursue more in the professional-fishing lines." Ozio added that there was "good money" to be made on the bass-fishing circuit.

  Similarly, when I start to drift out of sports television writing, I'm looking at the possibility of going into store-front window-display management, with an eye at reshaping the entire mannequin industry. There's good money to be made on the shopping-mall circuit.

- During the third quarter of a Bullets-Bucks NBA telecast on Home Team Sports regional cable, sideline reporter Kevin Grevey interviewed Miss Black America, Paula Gwynn. Grevey's only question to Gwynn was: "How does one become Miss Black America, outside of being very beautiful, of course?"

  Well, of course, the other key is being black.

- Chris Schenkel's interview of Del Ballard, Jr., after Ballard and Bob Benoit won the PBA Doubles Classic:

  Schenkel: "Congratulations, bridegroom."

  Ballard: "Thank you. I got married two weeks ago and people have always said that, you know, once you get married you've got to watch out, you won't bowl near as good but, hey, I'll tell you, it came through for me today."

  Conversely, my marriage took a nosedive *after* I started bowling.

- Before the Muhammad Ali-George Foreman fight in 1974, Ali said to Howard Cosell: "If I had a lower IQ, I could enjoy your interviews."

  Following that thought to its logical extreme, Ali

would've had to have the IQ of, say, an eggplant to enjoy any conversation with Mike Adamle or Lynn Swann.

- Seven Most Feared Words in TV Sports: "Hello once again, everybody, I'm Chris Berman . . ."

  Seven Second-Most Feared Words in TV Sports: "Describe him a bit for us, Mel." (Berman to Mel Kiper, Jr., at NFL draft.)

- From a long-running ad campaign: "Cable contributes to life."

  Yeah, right.

I Used to
Also Lend a Hand
to Mannix,
Which Might Be Why
He Went off the Air

Editor's Note: For years, unbeknownst to any of his read-ers, the author of this book has lived a double life. Most of the time, he is simply Norman Chad, Sports Television Colum-nist, and he sits at home monitoring and critiquing the endless panoply of video activity nationally. Other times, though— when developments warrant it—he becomes Chip Muldoon, Sports Television Detective, and he gets out and about trying to solve the endless panoply of TV-related crime nationally. What follows, adapted from the actual diaries of Chad/Muldoon, are details of two of his more compelling and complex cases from recent years:

He slapped her. She spat in his face.

"You're vile," he told her as he began to walk out.

She threw the *TV Guide* at him, and its force sent him tumbling to the floor. He settled in disgust next to the remote.

She apologized four or five times, offering to make him a TV dinner and to help him program the VCR to tape "Dobie Gillis" later that night.

He sat in silence, steamed. You could cut the tension in the room with a pair of those cable splicers favored by folks who try to get HBO for free. It had been the same old argument—she wanted to watch "Murphy Brown," he wanted to watch "Monday Night Football." Finally he spoke—and with such clarity and conviction that she could not mistake his intent.

"I hate you," he said, "and I'll kill you. You'll be dead because you don't deserve to live."

She swallowed hard and responded nervously. "Aw, come on, Marty, you talk like you mean it."

"I do mean it. You're a dead woman."

She laughed lightly, but she could not hide her anxiety. Marty Price had killed before over the clicker, and he would kill again.

The next day Sally called me. "Marty has a price on my head," she whimpered. "You've gotta help, Chip."

I didn't need the case, make no mistake about that. I've been earning what I need and more, and there was nothing more disruptive than working a contract case on a weekend.

"Will you do it?" she pleaded.

"Can you pay me?"

"What will it cost?"

"Everyone knows my rate, sweetheart," I told her. "Can you handle it?"

"If it will save my life," she said.

"You're a damn lucky broad," I sniffed. "Consider it saved."

I got off the phone and then called my bookie to place a

bet on the O'Hara fight. O'Hara was a drunken stiff, and I wasn't above making some money on a drunken stiff from time to time. It paid the bills.

Sally paid in advance—100 custom cigars from Havana, six cases of club soda, two London Fog overcoats and a deck of playing cards. It was my standard rate.

About a week later, she was killed by Marty Price's henchmen. Sometimes I help my clients, sometimes I don't. That's the nature of the business.

There was another time I was resting, watching the Bosox beat the Yankees on the rat box. I had emptied a couple of slugs into a card shark the night before when he had checked and raised the pot on me twice, and I was in no mood for anything. Nobody checks and tilts me, not in this town.

The phone rang. I hit the mute button on the remote—not a moment too soon; I'd about had my fill of Scooter Rizzuto—and picked up the receiver.

"Hi, it's Maggie," the voice on the other end of the line said.

"What do you know?" I asked with no particular emotion.

"It's my brother Louie," she said. "He's in a jam. He went in on a pay-per-view fight the other night with two other guys. They watched it at Louie's house. It was thirty bucks. He's supposed to meet Big Marv and Teddy G tonight to collect the double sawbuck they owe him, but he's going to get double-crossed and I can't reach him nowheres."

She spoke frantically, and it was hard to take it all in. She was talking faster than Delta Burke at a Taco Bell counter.

"OK, OK, calm down. What's the gig?"

"The payoff's tonight in the alley behind Market Place, but Marv's bringing his mugs to waste Louie."

"What time?"

"Ten o'clock."

"I'm there."

"You sure you can make it?" she said, haltingly.

"Cookie," I cooed, "I'm on the job. You're talking to Chip Muldoon, Sports Television Dick."

I grabbed my .45 and a couple of fat tobacco sticks and rushed out with the Red Sox ahead, 6–3.

I arrived just in time. There they were—the kid Louie, with three of Marv's mobsters, Petey, Scatface and Flick. They all had .38s aimed at the kid.

I jumped in front of Louie and stared at the punks menacingly until my contact lenses started watering.

"What? Huh? Is this . . . you are . . . hey!" Scatface mumbled.

"Still having trouble mastering the language, ain't that so, Scatface?" I said smugly.

"Ignore him," said Flick, the mastermind of the trio.

"You'd better listen and you'd better listen good," I commanded. "Louie had an agreement with Marv and Teddy G. I don't care if it turned out to be a bum fight. They watched it, so they owe for it. That's why they call it pay-per-view, gentlemen."

"Bullshit," Flick offered, fairly adamantly.

I broadened my stance in front of Louie. "There ain't going to be no killing tonight, boys," I announced. "You have to get through me to get to Louie."

Petey fired one shot into my arm and another into my rib cage. I crumpled to the ground and watched helplessly as they mowed down Louie with three shots to the chest.

"Damn," I moaned as they ran off.

I was in the hospital just two days and back at work by Tuesday. It's my job.

Future Vision:
AAAAAAAAAAHHH!!!

The year is 2010. (Let me just interrupt myself for a moment. Most of you, I assume, will be reading this book sometime in the 1990s—that is, if the publisher is a stand-up guy. Then again, if the publisher interprets contract law in a fashion similar to how my ex-wife interpreted our marital contract, then this book project just might end up on cocktail napkins and I'll be sure to owe somebody somewhere lots of money. Anyway, if you're reading this book and it's still the 1990s, fine. Proceed with care. But let's say you pick up this text in a library or you purchase it in a used-book store, and it happens to be sometime early in the twenty-first century. Hell, let's say it's 2009 or 2010. Well, what I'm going to have to ask you to do is skip this chapter because I'm going to be talking about what sports television might be like in 2010 and, frankly, I have no idea what's going to happen when 2010 rolls around. Now, that's OK for the folks reading this in the 1990s because, hey, they don't know what's going to happen either and they're just putting their blind faith in me, but for you folks picking up this volume in 2010, I'm going to look real, real stupid if you read this chapter. So let's do everybody a favor and go straight to the final chapter, and any of you who paid for this book, if you can find me, I'll give you a nominal refund because you didn't get your full money's worth by having to skip the next few pages.)

As I was saying, the year is 2010. (I need to interject one more small point, if I may. It is imperative that you folks who get this book in the 1990s actually read it in the 1990s, because if you buy it and don't read it until ten or fifteen years later, then you become just like the folks who get it for the first time in 2010. Thus, even though you bought it in the nineties, you'd have to skip these pages just like the 2010 group, which would mean that nobody—and I mean NOBODY—would be allowed to read this chapter. What would be the point of me even writing it then? I've never thought there was any reason to play a concert in the desert—particularly because the dry heat can have a miserable effect on the sound quality of a bass trombone—and I'm not going to start blowing my horn out there now.)

Anyway, the year in question is 2010. (Yeah, yeah, yeah, I know plenty of you are saying, "2010? Isn't that Arthur C. Clarke's bailiwick?" Sure, he wrote a book called *2010,* but it's not like he has exclusive properties on the whole damn year. Besides, that was 2010: The Book, and I'm just talking about 2010: The Chapter, not to mention he was writing science fiction and I'm writing sports television, and I think we all agree there is absolutely no relation between science fiction and sports television—well, other than Chris Berman, that is—so I'm just going to do my thing and if Mr. Big Shot Arthur C. Clarke wants to sue me, then, fine, I know my way around district court as well as the next guy.)

Let's start over, shall we?

The year is 2010. It is hot outside. Actually, it might be cold outside, but America wouldn't know. America is *inside,* with forty-eight-inch projection screens, interactive TVs, picture-in-picture options, microwave meals and, of course, The Remote.

The Remote will be to the twenty-first century what the septic tank was to the nineteenth. You won't have to move an inch in 2010 to go anywhere or do anything you want, save perhaps when you have a bowel movement. Then again, give technology enough time and that may be solved as well.

Here's a glimpse into the twenty-first century:

PAY-PER-VIEW: The good news is that you will be able to watch anything you want at any time of any day. The bad news is that you will pay for that privilege.

The good news is that everything will be available for viewing. The bad news is that nothing will be worth watching.

Pay-per-view scares folks, but it shouldn't. It's no different than toll roads. You pay as you go—if you use that highway, you pay for its maintenance; if you don't drive on that road, you don't get taxed for something that doesn't benefit you. What's the big hullabaloo over? This is America. You want something, you pay for it.

Actually, pay-per-view has been with us for a long, long time. The original pay-per-view? Those TV sets at airport terminals—you know, twenty minutes for a quarter—and, heck, I've never heard anybody complain about those babies.

HIGH-DEFINITION TELEVISION (HDTV): The standard American TV picture consists of 525 electronic lines. The HDTV picture will have 1,200 lines and offer a picture as sharp as 35-millimeter film; it will usher in a new era of picture quality.

On-screen people will appear to be actually in the same room as the viewer. (This should be a boon to the Playboy Channel.) On some of the more sophisticated, high-tech HDTV systems, the realism will be such that when, say, actors or athletes sweat during a tough scene or a tough game, perspiration actually will appear on your home TV screen. (Yes, there will be condensation on your TV set. Trust me.)

In limited cases—and I'm talking top-of-the-line HDTV models here—Dick Vitale will appear to be Satan himself.

SATELLITE DISHES: Gone will be the need for those rooftop and backyard pieces of high-priced china, replaced by satellite dishes so small, you'll be able to serve sushi on them. Individual satellites will even fit into your lunch boxes, allowing the return of daytime World Series games. (Schoolchildren used to rush home to watch these fall classics, but they'd miss some of the action because they'd be in class. No more. Kids now will be able to watch from the comfort of their school desks, juggling geography with Joe Garagiola.)

INTERACTIVE TV: You are the producer. You are the director. You are God with a clicker. You decide which camera angles you want. You decide which shots to replay.

You decide what the announcer tells you. You decide when to go to commercial.

Maybe even one day, *you* tell Dick Vitale he's fired.

You also shop, work, talk, bank and date through your TV. You live your entire life from the comfort of your couch. No traffic, no lines, no contact with anything but your color window on the world. (And because of the HDTV you can get hooked up to your interactive TV, the electronic bank teller will look so good, you'll want to start courting her from your very own home.)

You'll be able to vote from home. You'll be able to solve murder mysteries from home. You'll be able to heckle comedians from home. Of course, you'll also pay higher cable bills from home for all this two-way TV, but paying for pay-per-view should prepare you for that psychologically.

SURROUND SOUND: This is HDTV's audio partner, a technological marriage made, undoubtedly, in Japan.

If you can see it better, you may as well hear it better. To get the full effect of footage of, say, Niagara Falls, it would help if you virtually feel the water splashing against the rocks. A viewing system that combines HDTV, interactive TV and surround sound will allow the Falls to literally tumble into your lap. Traditional honeymoons will be as easy as one-two-three with your remote; why drive to Niagara Falls when you can have Niagara Falls come to you?

VCRs: Every videocassette recorder will be voice-activated. You just bark out a command, something like "Rewind!" or "Mute that bald ex–basketball coach who's screaming all the time!" and—*bang!!!*—your machine responds. VCRs will be more loyal than dogs and require less maintenance.

With certain VCRs, you will be able to program your own divorce.

INTERIOR DECORATING: The very look of your den or home entertainment area will change. Large wall hangings—you know, your huge Picassos and Monets and Pollocks—will be replaced by TV screens literally built into the structure of the room. When the TV is not being used, a variety of art can be displayed in that spot. (This is the same concept as rotating ad billboards at arenas and stadiums. In fact, certain companies might want to strike deals with private residences that entertain frequently for ad space on living room walls, producing something like, "IBM Presents The Greenbergers' Christmas Party, Sponsored by Diet Coke.")

VIRTUAL REALITY: Through state-of-the-art computer technology—using giant screens and advanced computer graphics and headsets containing sensors—Virtual Reality creates a lifelike experience for the user. Virtual Reality can simulate almost any environment—you can feel like you're flying a plane, you can feel like you're on Mars, you can feel like you're grocery-shopping, you can feel like you're in a salvageable marriage.

It's a spectacular electronic experience. Virtual Reality makes Nintendo look like checkers.

The key to this technology is that the viewer puts on a helmet that blocks his vision of the outside world. (Actually, Frank Gifford has done this successfully for more than forty years.) The helmet is connected to a computer, and a computer program projects images of another world before the viewer's eyes. This is called "location-based entertainment" and should not be confused with any ABC prime-time programming of the early 1970s.

RADIO: Radio? Radio? Are you kidding? Why will anyone ever listen to radio again?

In your car? Hah! There will be TV sets built into dashboards.

At the beach? Hah! There will be suntan lotions that produce TV images on your arm.

In the morning for the alarm? Hah! Chuck Woolery will come to your home and wake you in person.

While jogging? Hah! You're never going to move off your couch again.

(At least give radio credit—the car radio, that is—for being a forerunner to The Remote. Same concept: There are five or six buttons that you preset, then you go from station to station in search of something you want to hear. I had a friend once—I'll call him Howard Yablon because that was his name—who could recognize any song by hearing a single beat of it. Howard would hit that damn button every 1.3 seconds; I must've been in the car with him for three and a half years before I ever heard any Beatles song from start to finish.)

And now, a few other likely occurrences regarding sports television in 2010:

The Super Bowl goes for $24.95 ($26.95 if you want to electronically send in a play) on pay-per-view.

Frank Gifford is replaced on ABC's "Monday Night Football" by a replay machine with a computer-activated voice.

After a decade-long eating binge, John Madden's career as CBS's No. 1 NFL analyst and television's No. 1 pitchman ends abruptly as he sinks the boat and drowns during a take for a Tidy Bowl commercial.

SportsChannel America, frustrated by its attempts to compete with ESPN and thwarted in its merger effort with Prime Network as Prime SportsChannel, scales down its operation and is renamed SportsChannel Hackensack.

As part of ABC's budget cuts, the Goodyear blimp is replaced during football games by a teenaged hang glider, who takes Polaroid snapshots that are dropped into the sideline to a production assistant, who rushes the prints into the production truck for airing.

Brent Musburger, distraught that the younger Jim Nantz now broadcasts almost all the major events that he used to on CBS, takes Nantz hostage live from the Butler Cabin during the Masters.

Ronald Reagan, completing his second two-term presidency, joins Harry Caray as play-by-play announcer on WGN's Chicago Cubs telecasts.

The Olympics, in order to reap growing U.S. TV dollars, switches from quadrennial to semiannual, with the Winter Games scheduled during each February sweeps period and the Summer Games slated for each November sweeps period.

Ted Turner's TNT shows colorized versions of the 1927 World Series, the first Jack Dempsey-Gene Tunney fight and *Knute Rockne—All American*.

Dick Vitale pauses.

The automotive industry introduces the Toyota Telica GT, a two-door sports coupe featuring four TV monitors built into the dashboard with one-touch channel and volume control on the steering column.

ABC drops its contention that it is "recognized around the world as the leader in sports television," claiming instead to be "recognized around Hackensack as the leader in sports television." SportsChannel Hackensack sues.

The National Hockey League, determining that viewers' No. 1 complaint is they can't see goals when they're scored, switches to a larger, neon-lit puck modeled after Caesars Palace in Las Vegas.

High-definition TV instant replays (HDTVIR) become a standard officiating tool for professional sports. The NFL, in fact, dispenses with all on-field referees in favor of a "SkySuite EyeElite" crew that watches on 40-foot projection screens.

Bruce Springsteen introduces his latest music video, "500 Channels (and Nothin' On)" on the All-Michael 'n' Madonna cable network.

"Later" host Bob Costas and "Much Later" cohost Ahmad Rashad end a long-standing feud by rejoining NBC's "NFL Live" as co-anchors. Costas will do the program from St. Louis and Rashad, joined by an unspecified woman, will do it from Hollywood.

The NFL, after successful expansion to Europe, Japan and Atlantic City, reaches an agreement with Ohlmeyer Communications to televise a game from Mars without announcers.

With sales at a record high, Anheuser-Busch drops all network sports advertising temporarily because of a shortage of hops.

Marv Albert does not turn fifty. Ever.

Before I Get off
This Toll Road,
There Are a Few
Other Objects
I Need to Sideswipe

The waves swept in gently, a soft and lyrical backdrop to the setting sun. Sea gulls swooped over the fading day, dancing magically in the sky. The ocean air was intoxicating, a whiff of wet and wonderful life, with the rich beads of sand tickling the toes. It was a fleeting moment of unbridled beauty. I turned toward Monique, and while running my left hand through her smooth, silken hair, I reached back with my right hand and flicked on my battery-charged, solid-state, lightweight, quick-start, cable-ready-with-glare-free-sunscreen, auto-control-color Sony 5-inch TV set. The Buick Classic was under way, and I had to see it.

Ah, to be young and free and alive and able to watch TV golf at the beach, with a girl at your side and the ocean at your feet.

It is at moments such as these that I often ponder the whys and why nots of Our Existence. If, as often has been said, sports is a microcosm of life, then sports television must be a microcosm of life after death.

Thus, as a public service—well, maybe not so much a public service as a personal whim—I will take time out here to answer the most compelling and complex sports television questions of the day:

Q. Does sports television have as great an impact on this nation as many people say it does?
A. First there was the wheel, then the telegraph, then air-conditioning. They set the tone for industrial America up until 1950. Then came microwave ovens, disposable razors, 7-Elevens and sports television, which have ruled our lives ever since.

Q. Did any single event trigger the sports television boom?
A. Howard Cohen, a New York lawyer, decided to become Howard Cosell, a New York sportscaster.

Q. How come so much golf is on TV?
A. Because it's a lousy radio sport.

Q. Why do beer companies advertise so much on sports television?
A. Why do merchants near beaches stock so much suntan lotion?

Q. How old is Marv Albert?
A. Remember those song lyrics "I love you more today

than yesterday, but not as much as tomorrow"? Well, Marv may be a bit older today than he was yesterday, but he won't necessarily be any older tomorrow.

Q. What are the main elements that go into most network sports decision-making on programming, schedule changes and production elements and into most professional leagues' thinking on how and when to televise their games?
A. Money.

Q. Will NFL games ever go off free TV?
A. See previous question and answer.

Q. Do people really watch professional bowling in the great numbers that the Nielsens say they do?
A. If the Summer or Winter Olympics ever had to go head-to-head against bowling on a weekly basis, no one ever would've heard of Mark Spitz, Peggy Fleming or Mary Lou Retton.

Q. How do they always know where the players' wives are sitting?
A. They don't. They just pick fairly attractive women and identify them as they please. Since both the player and his wife are usually at the game, they don't get to see the telecast; thus, no one is the wiser.

Q. What's the deal with all these British commentators on TV golf coverage over the years?
A. As part of an unusual U.S.-British trade agreement, we are required to place at least one whispering British commentator on every network golf telecast. In return, we don't ever have to eat any of their food.

Q. What phrase or expression is most associated with NBC Sports?
A. "Ladies and gentlemen, we are experiencing technical difficulties. Please stand by . . ."

Q. Why do announcers always wear a tuxedo at figure skating events?
A. Would you want to be caught on-camera before an ice dancing competition in a leisure suit?

Q. OK, then, why do announcers also always wear tuxedos when broadcasting these big pay-per-view fights?
A. Well, boxing matches are a bit like weddings: Two people get together for the same purpose and end up beating each other half to death.

Q. Whatever happened to "Mutual of Omaha's Wild Kingdom"?
A. It was replaced by Dick Vitale.

Q. How exactly are the Nielsen ratings determined?
A. The A. C. Nielsen Co. used to use a small, scientific cross section of American homes to gauge what the nation at large was watching. Because of recent financial constraints, though, Nielsen now just monitors the viewing habits of seven individuals living in a sixties-style group house in Scranton, Pennsylvania.

Q. Do any network play-by-play broadcasters wear an earring while on air?
A. At press time, no play-by-play man was wearing an earring on air. A handful of the married announcers, though, do wear a wedding ring from time to time.

Q. Why do sports and news anchors always shuffle the papers in front of them when they finish a broadcast?
A. It's easier than picking up the TelePrompTer.

Q. Willow Bay?
A. Willow Bay.

Q. CBS and NBC "scramble" their signal on NFL telecasts to prevent satellite dish owners from picking up those games illegally. How come ABC does not have to do this?
A. ABC, disdainful of costly new technology, in effect already scrambles its "Monday Night Football" signal by using Frank Gifford as a broadcaster.

Q. What would happen to "Monday Night Football" if it went off the air?
A. It would be syndicated in reruns, likely on Nick at Nite.

Q. Why is cable theft a crime?
A. Possibly because prosecutors have never watched cable.

Q. What are the Seven Wonders of the World?
A. TNT's on-air cast for its pregame NFL "Stadium Show."

Q. Is chess a better radio or TV sport?
A. Actually, because of the intricacies and pacing of each match, chess play-by-play usually is best conveyed through letter-writing among individuals.

Q. Why are the screens at movie theaters getting smaller and the screens on TV sets getting larger?
A. This is a natural progression, since it's easier to find a parking spot at home.

Q. What is photosynthesis?
A. Photosynthesis? How did that question get in here? Who do I look like, Pierre Curie? I'm not even sure how my cable works.

Q. If a "Q score" reflects a broadcaster's recognizability and likability, what reflects a broadcaster's ability?
A. The "TNT score," derived by subtracting the number of years someone works for Turner Broadcasting from the total number of years that person has worked in the business. (Zero is the lowest possible score.)

Q. What products does John Madden not endorse?
A. Madden endorses or is in the midst of negotiations to endorse every product in the American marketplace today, other than those products currently endorsed by Michael Jordan.

Q. What exactly is the Emergency Broadcast System?
A. Anytime a network is forced to use Mike Adamle to broadcast a sporting event.

Q. Why do the networks continue to hire marquee ex-jocks as game analysts?
A. Network honchos believe that if Don Nottingham and Phil McConkey are working as commentators on, say, a Super Bowl, while, in the same time period, O. J. Simpson and Frank Gifford are working as commentators on a taped flag football game featuring all-star teams composed of top certified public accountants and top auto insurance adjusters, many of us will watch the latter telecast just to hear Juice and Giff. Really, that's what they think.

Q. Is there a reason that anytime one grazes through cable TV with a remote, there always seems to be a sporting event on every other channel at any hour of the day?

A. Yes. It's because, generally speaking, there *is* a sporting event on cable TV on every other channel at any hour of the day.